THRIVE
Applying Biblical and Quantum Energy Principles to Live a Transformed Life

Robin Perry Braun, M.Psy.

Scripture quotations marked AMP are taken from the Amplified® Bible, Copyright © 1954, 1958, 1962, 1964, 1965, 1987 by The Lockman Foundation. Used by permission. (www.Lockman.org) Scripture quotations marked ESV are taken from the English Standard Version (ESV) The Holy Bible, English Standard Version. ESV® Text Edition: 2016. Copyright © 2001 by Crossway Bibles, a publishing ministry of Good News Publishers. Scripture quotations marked EXB are taken from The Expanded Bible, Copyright © 2011 by Thomas Nelson, Inc. Used by permission. All rights reserved. Scripture quotations marked NASB are taken from the New American Standard Bible, Copyright ©1960, 1962, 1963, 1968, 1971, 1972, 1973, 1975, 1977, 1995 by The Lockman Foundation, La Habra, Calif. All rights reserved. Scripture quotations marked NIV are taken from the Holy Bible, New International Version®. NIV®, Copyright © 1973, 1978, 1984 by International Bible Society. Used by permission of Zondervan. All rights reserved worldwide. Scripture quotations marked NKJV are taken from the New King James Version®, Copyright © 1982 by Thomas Nelson. Used by permission. All rights reserved. Scripture quotations marked KJ21 are taken from the 21st Century King James Version Bible, Copyright © 1994 by Deuel Enterprises, Inc.

Bluewater Publications
BWPublications.com
Printed in the United States

This work is based on the author's personal perspective. It is the author's intention to give full credit to sources used in the research process of this publication. A full bibliography can be found at the end of this book.

Editors – Rachel Davis & Sandi Harvey
Interior Design – Rachel Davis
Cover Design – Terri Dilley
Managing Editor – Angela Broyles

ACKNOWLEDGMENTS

It becomes difficult to name all the people who have impacted you over the course of thirty years. (There are just so many!) My passion for the content of this book was ignited first by the lifetime work of John and Paula Sandford, perhaps two of the boldest pioneers in inner healing ever. More contemporarily, I have learned from many pioneers in quantum physics healing and Bible application. God supernaturally led me to them and their work to guide my calling and destiny. (These figures are noted in the bibliogrography.)

Many thanks to Rachel Davis, Sandi Harvey, Dawn Egan and Connie Blackburn for going above the call of duty in helping to edit with excellence. Thanks to Angela Broyles, my publisher, for her belief in the message and encouragement. And most of all, thank you to my Lord Jesus and Heavenly Papa for guiding me in this incredible journey of healing and transformation, never leaving me even for a moment.

TABLE OF CONTENTS

INTRODUCTION

Since I wrote the first edition of *A Believer's Guide to the Law of Attraction* in 2013, much has changed in the general population's understanding of quantum physics and the principles they convey. While many Christians are hesitant to embrace these principles, the general population seems to more readily grasp the concepts of quantum physics. It becomes easier to discuss something that has become more widely known and accepted, even in the past six years. There still remains, however, a shroud of mystery around these principles.

Are they New Age?

Do they align with scripture?

Is it something that should even be on my radar and if so, why?

As I uncover these principles, I hope to answer those questions and bring life and application in a transformational way.

By teaching and applying these principles, I have experienced amazing results – not only in my own life, but also in the lives of my clients. What was once theory about an applied science has proven to work out in dozens of people's lives I have observed and been party to. I have witnessed firsthand many clients experiencing:

- Transformed health and/or weight loss
- Depression and anxiety lifted
- Business expansion and finding they are attracting what they want
- Relationships transformed
- Addictions abated
- A general tangible improvement in the quality of life, peace, and joy

- A deeper and more tangible connection in their relationship with the Lord and belief in His love
- Relationships with estranged children restored
- Family relationship dynamics shifted overall and more...

This new and expanded edition is filled with life-changing stories and applications.

In this new leg of my journey, I have taught and trained people on how to find personal freedom and come alongside others on their freedom journey. Through workshops and speaking, I educate people on how to raise their individual and corporate vibration.

Though less frequent, there are still times when I teach on this topic to other Christians and they have no idea what I am saying. There is, however, a growing consensus of solid theologians and scientists who can explain things in more simple terms, thereby making the learning curve easier. While the Christian church historically throws out anything other streams of spirituality have embraced (for fear of being deceived), truth ultimately comes from God and may be expressed through channels unfamiliar to us, our worldview, or our particular denominational vantage point. If only individual believers had the security in their walk with God and intimacy with the Holy Spirit to mine truth from all sources, validate it with scripture, and understand its application in our lives. God wants us to heal and mature. He releases revelation in the season it is needed, but He often confounds the boxes and formulas we create. He may choose to use "the foolish to confound the wise" (1 Corinthians 1:27). We can become pharisaical if we think God only speaks through and gives understanding to born-again believers. If that's the case, we need to throw out much of the minute-by-minute science and technology we apply every day.

My own struggles and those in my marriage led me to seek answers I had not found in the previous multitude of modalities I had researched, trained in, or read about. I knew, though, there were tools somewhere.

In high school, I struggled with my self-worth and became obsessed with my body image. This led to a long battle with anorexia/bulimia and thus my desire to seek out personal healing and transformation. After a few years of tenaciously pursuing it, I was completely healed and set free from this obsession and eating disorder (which is very rare, statistically speaking).

In 1986, I accepted Christ as my savior in a church service in Atlanta. I have been a student of inner healing and Christian counseling for the past 30+ years. I hold a Bachelors degree in Psychology and Biblical Studies and a Masters degree in Clinical Psychology. I am in the dissertation process for my PhD in Integrated Medicine. I am certified in Elijah House, Restoring the Foundations, Vision Life Ministries, and Exchanged Life Christian Counseling. I completed the requirements for a Licensed Professional Counselor in the state of Texas, but have since been led in a different direction. I have used these certifications and modalities collectively in a variety of Christian prayer and counseling settings including an International Sexual Addiction Ministry, a Christian Inpatient Adolescent Treatment Center, and many churches and parachurch ministries. I have a thriving private practice and have created a certified holistic energy modality where I invest in training other practitioners. I believe God designed our incredible bodies to stay healthy and heal themselves, if we can identify the source of stress that is causing sickness and remove it. He does indeed heal miraculously, but the disease/illness may return if we don't find the root cause.

It has been my life's pursuit to find the best healing modalities for the wounds in most Christians. While I have seen many instant healings of physical issues, I have witnessed few truly instantaneous healings of wounded hearts. Rather, these seem to occur little by little in relational settings. Since the wounding typically occurs in relationships, God tends to bring healing in relational ways.

In my own journey and from observing that of many others, I have discovered missing pieces in many of the therapy modalities I have seen and experienced. I believe that the truths behind the Law of Attraction, which I will correlate to Biblical principles, provide some very significant missing pieces to the healing of the whole person—body, soul, and spirit. My desire is to shed some light on these principles. Ultimately, my goal is not only to educate you on the Biblical validity of quantum physics principles, but also to show how useful the Law of Attraction can be in application to the wounds of our souls and hearts.

In preparation for writing this book, I bought *Quantum Physics for Dummies*. What an oxymoron! I expected a book using layman's terms of the principles about quantum physics I had learned from other avenues. What I discovered was a book that required an IQ of at least 190 to even decipher the formulas and code on most of the pages. I suppose in the field of quantum physics the term "dummy" is relative.

Quantum physics is one of the most researched topics currently ranked on search engines. Consequently, this is a "now" book containing relevant teaching on a topic many are currently researching. Within these pages, I believe you will gain understanding regarding the Law of Attraction but, more specifically, you will find a Biblical basis for its veracity AND a practical way to apply it to your own life for radical transformation.

It saddens me how the metaphysical church recognizes the power in all truth and applies it to their lives, yet are rejected by mainstream Christianity because they may be too broad and inclusive for our comfort level and theology. Scripture is our plumb line, even if we don't all agree on various Biblical doctrines. The Holy Spirit reveals truth to our innermost parts if we will spend our life seeking to know Him at this deep level of intimacy. I believe the church's core issue is not primarily a problem of doctrines, but an intimacy disorder (at least in my American Church experience). We desperately try to substitute head knowledge for the living relationship with the Holy Spirit.

As believers in the Lord Jesus Christ, filled with the Holy Spirit, we have access to the clearest, most direct pathway to truth and the power of God. Consequently, we should all be experiencing physical, emotional, and spiritual wellness. We should be walking in peace and joy. Proverbs 4:18 (English Standard Version) says:

But the path of the righteous is like the light of dawn, which shines brighter and brighter until full day.

In my experience, Christians seem to have as many, if not more, problems than the rest of the world. The Bible tells us to be salt and light to the world (Matthew 5:13-16). We are supposed to stand out, look different, and make a difference. Based on my years of observation, Christians as a whole are not very salty and our light is not as bright as past eras. This is apparent in a declining church base, a lack of evidence of the fruit of the Spirit in the lives of the general population of believers, and Christians suffering from as many health issues as non-Christians. It has been my life's pursuit to know why this is the case and be an instrument of healing.

CHAPTER 1
BASICS OF QUANTUM PHYSICS
AND THE LAW OF ATTRACTION

I received the only 'D' I ever had on a test in my eleventh grade physics class. Mr. Biedryzski (buh-drizz-skee) was about a hundred years old and showed us movies from the fifties (this was the early 80's). Most of us fell asleep within five minutes of the movie starting. We called this phenomenon "The Biedryzski Syndrome." We thought we had cleverly made this up only to find out that my brother and his classmates had coined the same term for the same thing some nine years earlier. The sudden onset of sleepiness was a classic symptom of attempting to grasp physics. So, while I aced calculus and was ranked third in a class of 550 students, physics eluded me. In an effort to not repeat the Biedryzski curse, I have made this section short and easy to understand. If you find yourself nodding off, instead of putting your head down, give yourself a quick slap. I promise this will be short and painless. You might even think you are smart by the end of this chapter!

Like Newtonian physics, quantum physics cannot be easily taught or explained in purely scientific terms. I am certain a minimum IQ of genius is required to understand the math. You can find short videos on YouTube that do the best job at keeping it understandable. Grasping these basic paradigmatic principles will alter the way you view the world, thought, speech, time, and life. Everything shared is easily verified online, so you can research in depth if you desire. The topic is quite fascinating.

The definition of *quantum physics*, a.k.a. *quantum mechanics* is the study of the smallest particles of physical phenomena. Specifically, it looks at atomic and subatomic particles and waves from all sources of matter. Research in this field has been a main focus of grant money over the past couple of decades and even more recently as technology has produced methods for accurately measuring movement of small particles. For our purposes, I will detail three basic truths that have now been proven scientifically. These truths will then be applied practically throughout this book.

Truth #1

The first truth is that *everything is made up of atoms and particles, which are energy*. Scientists have known this to be true for decades, hence why you and I learned about it in middle/high school, but there has never been much talk about the conclusions. If everything is comprised of atoms, then all humans are made up of energy and only a small part of us is actually solid matter. We know that the majority of an atom is simply empty space in motion. In fact, did you realize over 99.99% of an atom is space? The illusion of having more matter is only because it is in motion. For example, if you move a flashing light between two points quickly, it gives the illusion of a line, but in reality, it is a series of dots.

So this:

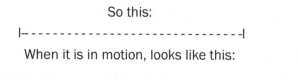

When it is in motion, looks like this:

This means that you and I are essentially a hologram. Years ago, when I saw the movie *The Matrix* for the first time, something shifted deep inside me that I could not articulate. Somehow I knew, maybe for the first time, that the world I saw was an illusion and the real world was the spirit realm. It shifted my faith and I often meditate on this concept when I am "stuck in the trees and can't see the forest." Do you ever find yourself in this same place? Those great heroes of faith whom I admire seem to live this idea and are not moved by circumstances or what they see. Remember Hebrews 11:1 (King James Version):

Now **faith** is the substance **of things** hoped for, **the evidence of things not seen**.

Imagine if we could truly observe our reality as a hologram, knowing that the only true reality is spiritual (or quantum) and what we experience is a result of our consciousness (individual and collective). I imagine we would live life very differently.

Historically, Hollywood seems to have a pulse on what God is doing in the universe and they often (knowingly and unknowingly) prophesy about it. If we look at many movies from the past years, we find the topics of time travel, dream states, other realities, and more. Wrapping our brains around the idea that we are more than 99.99% empty space is not just material for blonde jokes. Given the current movement towards energy medicine and healing, it simply makes good scientific sense to learn more about this idea that we are made up of energy. Learning a new paradigm about vibration and energy is exciting, but also challenging because it seems to violate most of our past paradigms. I encourage you to brave this journey as you see how quantum physics is grounded in the Word of God. I am confident God will bring revelation to you along the way. I still don't have my finite brain wrapped around most of the quantum physics discoveries, yet just like eating a 20 ounce t-bone steak, I take one small bite at a time.

With the recent development of technology that can measure the frequency of various objects and living things, we have come to find that the human body vibrates between 62-68 MHz when it is healthy. This is an accumulation of the various organs of the body as each is slightly different. Sickness starts to occur when the overall frequency begins to drop below 62. Cancer vibrations are known to drop the overall frequency and death occurs when the frequency drops below 35 MHz. Keep this concept of cumulation in mind, it is the key to making this paradigm shift.[i]

To repeat, **Truth #1 says we are all made up of atoms and thus made up of energy**.

Truth #2

The second truth is that *all energy vibrates and gives off a frequency that is measured at a certain wavelength.*

Different energies create different wavelengths or frequencies. High frequency means the peaks of the wavelengths are close together and occur more often. Low frequency means the peaks of the wavelengths are farther apart and occur less often.

Wavelength is not usually measured in meters (m), but in smaller parts of a meter (smaller than a millimeter or the width of a dime). Frequency is the number of cycles of a wave to pass some point in a second. The units of frequency are cycles per second, or Hertz (Hz). Radio stations have frequencies that are typically equal to the station number times 1,000,000 Hz. For instance, if a radio station has the FM band of 94.9, then it has a frequency of 94.9 million Hz. Did you know that electromagnetic waves can not only be described by their wavelength, but also by their energy and frequency? **All three of these things are related to each other mathematically**.

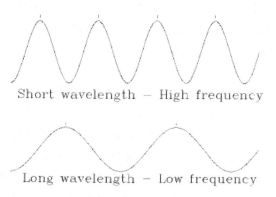

Short wavelength – High frequency

Long wavelength – Low frequency

Sound frequency has been studied and understood for many decades. When you turn on your radio to 94.9, that is a frequency your radio is finding. That radio station is sending its signal out on that specific frequency. When you tune into the same frequency, you pick up the signal. The frequency can only travel so many miles depending on the strength of the projector/tower that is sending the signal. Televisions and cell phones operate on the same principle. Satellites in space do as well, but are much more powerful and can cover greater territory. We use frequency technology every day, but many of us take it for granted. Humans also emit and receive frequencies 24/7, but are not aware of it unless taught to be aware.

We all know dogs hear a greater range of frequency than the human ear does. That is why a dog whistle agitates a dog, yet we hear nothing. Our eardrum does not pick up the frequency of the whistle, so it does not vibrate when the whistle is blown. How amazing is our human body that our ear works like a receiver sending signals to the brain to turn wavelengths into words, harmonies, etc.? God created us as a walking satellite, sending and receiving signals or frequencies. Did you know Einstein knew this at the turn of the century? He theorized that the human brain operated as a two-way satellite, sending and receiving signals.[ii] Newer studies of the pineal gland show it actually does function as a satellite transmitter and receiver.[iii]

Our eyes also see because of frequencies and colors have different wavelengths. A rainbow is light separated into its different frequencies. Our finely tuned eyes can distinguish hundreds, even thousands, of nuances in color along with shape and size. Both our ears and eyes function as receptors of frequency.

Did you know smells also have distinct frequencies? Our nose picks up the frequency and transmits it to the brain. Did you know in the field of aromatherapy different essential oils (oils made from the essence of a plant, flower, etc.) directly affect the brain by the frequency they transmit? Our brain reacts to these frequencies by sending different signals to the body. The scientific developments in this field contain facts worthy of research. This is another example of areas the metaphysical and New Age arenas have embraced for years. The mainstream population is only now accepting this because it can be proven scientifically. So, **truth #2 is that all energy vibrates and gives off a frequency.**

Truth #3

The third truth is that *wavelengths or frequencies attract similar or like wavelengths or frequencies.* They are magnetic in nature, so they attract like frequencies as a magnet does. So, high frequency Hz attract like high frequency Hz and low frequency Hz attract like low frequency Hz. While it is not my intent to go into detail on the quantum mechanics of particles and wavelengths, the following passage gives some scientific explanation of the correlation between quantum physics and the "like attracts like" principle for those who want to understand it from a more scientific basis:

Those who protest are totally right that like-charges repel each other in Quantum physics – positive charges repel positive charges, for example – that's the electromagnetic force.

But, there is another force that is 100 times stronger than the electromagnetic force, and physicists call that the "strong force" – it's the force that holds the nucleus of every atom together. The nucleus of an atom is composed of neutrons and positive-charged protons, which normally repel each other completely.

Dr. Hideki Yukawa (Nobel prize in physics) discovered way back in 1935 (and it was confirmed in 1947 and accepted as fact ever since then), that neutrons and protons in the nucleus of the atom (together called nucleons) constantly emit "virtual particles" called "mesons" and that they exchange these mesons with another nucleon (proton) or with themselves, and this interaction is what creates the "strong force" that holds the nucleus of the atom (and therefore all of physical reality) together.

In order to create this strong force, protons (nucleons) emit the virtual meson particles toward other like-particles in order to attract them into, or keep them in, the nucleus of an atom. The action and result that is created by this exchange of virtual particles among like-particles is that "strong force" itself – the strong

11

force would not exist without this exchange of virtual particles.

Thoughts are virtual particles. An atom, particles, everything that exists has intelligence and memory. Virtual particles are the thoughts of particles. Attraction would not exist without thoughts, the exchange of thoughts, and the exchange of virtual particles.

That's how like attracts like - by the exchange of information, virtual particles, thoughts – on the atomic level, and on the human interaction level. And, this attraction force is 100 times stronger than the repelling force.

*Some say there can be no connection between the atomic level and thought, between particles and human interaction, that virtual particles cannot be thought, and that there is no proof for the **Law of Attraction** in Quantum physics.*

I did not make it up!! And this is not new information. A particle, whether it's a virtual particle or a real physical particle, does not even exist until an observer (i.e. a person) focuses a thought upon it and causes it to appear from nowhere. Before that moment, it was only a probability, a specific frequency, raw information that had no locality and no form. The act of a thought brought it into existence. And, raw information itself is a thought (intelligence), and a thought (intelligence) is raw information. **These are all commonly accepted principles in Quantum physics.**

The concept that a thought (human interaction) creates particles, that a thought creates physical form, has been put out in theory and later confirmed in research by many people. Among those theories are those of Max Planck in 1900 (quantum hypothesis), Niels Bohr in 1924 (probability waves), Werner Heisenberg in 1927, Richard Feynman in 1949, J.S. Bell in 1964, David Bohm in 1970. There are many others, then and now. [iv]

According to Kevin Trudeau, best-selling author and teacher on the law of attraction, this is not new information. Trudeau, in his course

"Your Wish Is Your Command," shares that the information and practices related to quantum physics and the law of attraction theory have been kept secret for decades by the elite (or ultra-wealthy).[v]

Again, wrapping your brain around this is like eating a 20 ounce steak. Quantum physics scientists agree across the board that "like attracts like" and that is good enough for me. As I explain the Biblical principles later on, you will see the Word of God says the same thing.

We Are All Made Up of Light

The first truth established that all matter is made up of energy. Again, science proved many years ago that all matter is made up of atoms. We learned in middle/high school that atoms are made up of smaller particles like photons, electrons, neutrons, and quarks in motion. Atoms are only a very small percentage of actual physical matter; the rest is just space (more than 99.99%). Quantum physics tells us that light or electromagnetic energy holds together and makes up these particles. Therefore, all matter is actually some form of light or energy. You and I are made up of light.

The Bible tells us that God is light and we are made in His image and likeness. We are the LIGHT of the world. Our natural mind has a hard time wrapping itself around this idea. How can we be light? Light can shine through a window, but we cannot physically walk through a window. Even though science declares these things alike, our bodies cannot act as light does. This concept cannot be seen in the natural, but can be believed through faith. As we move into the principles of energy that are also true for the body, keep in mind this idea that everything is frequency, vibration, light, and energy. This new paradigm is necessary to revisit in order to make a shift in your health and life.

The Human Body Gives Off Frequencies

Because, like everything else, we are made up of waves of energy, then, like everything else, we vibrate and give off a frequency. The following blog on electromagnetic frequencies states:

According to Dr. Robert O. Becker in his book, <u>The Body Elec-</u>
<u>tric</u>, the human body has an electrical frequency and that much
about a person's health can be determined by it. Frequency is
the measurable rate of electrical energy flow that is constant
between any two points. Everything has frequency.

Dr. Royal R. Rife found that every disease has a frequency. He
has found that certain frequencies can prevent the development
of disease and that others would destroy diseases. Substances
of higher frequency will destroy diseases of lower frequency.

In 1992, Bruce Taino of Taino Technology, an independent divi-
sion of Eastern State University in Cheny, Washington, built the
first frequency monitor in the world. Taino has determined that
the average frequency of a healthy human body during the day-
time is 62 to 68 Hz. When the frequency drops, the immune sys-
tem is compromised. If the frequency drops to 58 Hz, cold and
flu symptoms appear; at 55 Hz, diseases like Candida take hold;
at 52 Hz, Epstein Bar and at 42 Hz, Cancer. Taino's machine
was certified as 100 percent accurate and is currently being
used in the agricultural field today.

The study of frequencies raises an important question con-
cerning the frequencies of substances we eat, breathe, and
absorb. Many pollutants have low frequencies and cause the
body's healthy frequencies to be lowered and weakened. Pro-
cessed or canned food has a frequency of zero and tends to
lower healthy frequencies within the body towards degenera-
tive diseases. Fresh produce has up to 15 Hz; dry herbs from
12 to 22 Hz; and fresh herbs from 20 to 27 Hz. Essential oil
frequencies start at 52 Hz and go as high as 320 Hz; which is
the frequency of Rose Oil. **These higher frequencies create an**
environment in which disease, bacteria, virus, fungus, can-
cer, etc., CANNOT live... [vi]

In later chapters, I will go into detail about understanding a new
world paradigm of frequency. For example, studies show that positive

emotions create higher Hz or wavelength frequencies while negative emotions give off lower Hz. By the same notion, thoughts and intent have the same effect. Negative thoughts produce lower Hz than positive thoughts. There is a great deal of scientific evidence in the past few years validating these findings and the evidence can be easily researched. Applied kinesiology, also know as "muscle testing," is a technique which determines a positive or negative flux of frequency. Lie detectors are also based on this energy theory. Muscle testing has now been validated after millions of independent studies to verify its validity and reliability. Persons in a positive emotional state or thinking positive thoughts registered much higher on a strength scale than persons in a negative state.

In the book *Power vs. Force*, Dr. David Hawkins goes into great detail about these implications. This book also explores in detail the vibration of different situations and environments.[vii]

Have you ever entered a room and just felt bad? You were probably picking up a low frequency. Demonic or evil situations give off a low frequency while the anointing of God gives off a high frequency. I also believe the presence of angels gives off a really high frequency. The implications of this in a healing environment are that releasing negative trapped emotions results in a higher overall frequency and the ability to choose to think more positive thoughts, changing the subconscious negative belief systems. My private practice and certified modality, **Integrated Life Process,** is based on this principle of frequency. More information can be found at **IntegratedLifestrategies.com**. If you research the Emotion Code by Dr. Bradley Nelson, he is forerunner in establishing this concept of emotional energy release. These concepts will be further discussed throughout this book.

It is recognized in the medical profession as a proven fact that physical health is directly related to thought-life and emotions, and that more than 80% of all illness is related to emotional and mental stress. There are many books on this topic. The allopathic medical model acknowledges this truth but it still focuses only on treating symptoms and not identifying roots.

Experiments of Dr. Masaru Emoto

Over the past few years, the experiments of Dr. Masaru Emoto have gained much acclaim. Dr. Emoto took water samples from a polluted river in Japan and subjected them to different treatments. He subjected some to classical music, some to heavy metal music, some to prayers, some to negative critical words, and some to positive encouraging words. On some samples, he taped words on the vial that held the water, but nothing was spoken (no sound waves, just thoughts). After an equal period of time, he quickly froze the water and cut samples from the ice to place under a dark field microscope. The resulting pictures on the next page are from one of these experiments.[viii]

The outcome of this experiment demonstrated that positive thoughts, words, and emotions affected the molecular structure of water in a beautiful, structured way, and that negative thoughts, words, and emotions affected the same water samples in a destructive way. Humans are more than 60% water. The point is that our words and what we listen to impact our very cells and DNA. Stop for a minute and think about everything you have said and thought about today. What kind of water crystals were you creating? Even more surreal and scary is the proof that thoughts, feelings, and emotions have a definite physical impact on our bodies as well. Most medical experts will agree now that the cause of most diseases is rooted in emotions and negative belief systems.

So, the human body is made up of energy that gives off frequencies or wavelengths. Our thoughts, feelings, and emotions on both a conscious and subconscious level can create either harmony or chaos within our body. They also give off a correlating vibration or wavelength that extends outside of us. Sounds, music, foods, smells, and other people generate frequencies that directly affect ours. Disease can only exist in a low vibration environment. This paradigm is now proven from many scientific sources. Do these facts make you hungry to know more about this?

Before　　**After**

Effect on Water of
Immune Vibration

500 people sending
positive thoughts
to bottled water

Prayer over Water

The pictures above show what the water looked like before and after the particular stimulus. The positive stimuli created beautiful snowflake patterns.

the word Angel　the word Peace　the word Spirit　the words You disgust me　the words You foc

Air on a G string by Bach　Imagine by John Lennon　Amazing Grace　Photo of Dolphins　Photo of Lotus

When the stimuli were positive songs, intentions, and images, the results were harmonious, ordered crystal structures. When the stimuli were hateful and disordered, the results were chaotic and disharmonious.

CHAPTER 2
THE LAW OF ATTRACTION AND
THE SECRET

The Secret was a best-selling novel and movie in the mid 2000s that introduced the law of attraction to the general population. Recapping chapter one of *The Secret*, we see the following new paradigm of viewing our world and everything inside this world from a quantum perspective:

- Everything is energy.
- All energy vibrates and has a frequency; these concepts are interchangeable.
- Frequency is measurable.
- High frequency attracts high frequency magnetically.
- Low frequency attracts low frequency magnetically.
- Sounds, words, thoughts, colors, and everything have a fre quency that impacts and alters whatever it touches.

Then, the law of attraction can simply be understood with the phrase "like attracts like." The frequency we emit has a certain wavelength. Positive emotions like love, joy, happiness, and gratitude have a high frequency or a short distance between wave peaks. Positive thoughts and words give off the same positive frequencies. Harmonious melodies are high frequency wavelengths. Healthy foods, supplements, oils, and natural products have a high frequency effect on the body. The opposite is true for negative emotions, thoughts, words, unnatural foods (like white refined sugar), pollution, chemicals, toxins, and so on.[ix]

As previously discussed, these waves attract using the strong force principle. High frequencies attract high frequencies and low frequencies attract low frequencies. In essence, love attracts love and hate attracts hate. The field of attraction coaching takes this principle in all of its many nuances and applications and helps people learn to change their lives by changing their thoughts and feelings. In the controversial book, *The Secret,* Rhonda Byrne compiles lists of principles from successful attraction coaches and teachers.[x] While many Christians rejected the ideas based on their presentation, in hindsight, we now understand that she was presenting scientific, tested, and proven energy theory.

Summary of *The Secret*

The law of attraction was made popular by Byrne's book and was quickly made into a movie that sold very successfully. At that time, information about the laws of quantum physics had not become as mainstream or easily accessible as in recent years. Readers of *The Secret* looked at these principles from a strictly metaphysical stance and while many embraced them, a large majority of both Christians and non-Christians alike wrote this principle off as a New Age or metaphysical principle. *The Secret* is considered by many as a text manual for the law of attraction. The bullet points below highlight much of its application of the law of attraction.

- Like attracts like in word, emotion, and thought.
- Thoughts become things. We can attract and create.
- The universe was made from thoughts.
- We "order" what we want with our thoughts. If we do this deliberately then we can expect our desires to manifest.
- People think about what they don't want, which attracts that to them.
- Thoughts are always planting seeds.
- Feelings let us know what we are thinking.
- We can make a choice to change our thoughts and then deliberately add emotions to them.
- If we think love, we will get love back.
- Believe that the universe is for you and then have faith.

- When you try to figure out how what you want is going to manifest then you emit doubt.
- The practice of the law of attraction is feeling what it is like to have it all now.
- Attracting may require action, but it will be joyful to do it.
- Every possibility for your life already exists, right now, in an other dimension outside of time. Time only exists in this dimension. Doubt keeps us from manifesting what we want in this dimension.
- Size doesn't matter, it is as easy for the universe to produce a million dollars as a dollar.
- Ask, believe, receive.
- Practice gratitude.
- Expect what you want.
- Visualize. There is no difference in the brain between actual experience and visualizing an experience.
- Giving joyfully feels good and creates attraction. Giving sacrificially is operating in fear or with resentment.
- Think abundance. Don't say things like: "I can't afford it."
- Abundance is not just money, it is in all areas and includes inner peace.
- The law of attraction includes thoughts about oneself.
- Disease and sickness are a by-product of how you think about yourself.
- Words and thoughts create your world. If you use the word "battle," then expect a battle.
- When we focus on negative things, they expand.
- We determine our destiny based on our perspective about it.[xi]

There are other, more specific points in *The Secret*. This list details what I feel are the key ones. Each chapter gives examples of people using the law of attraction in their lives.

While the allusion is not made, it turns out the title word "secret" is the same reference that, according to Kevin Trudeau in his tape series

"Your Wish is Your Command" has been used for decades by the wealthy to continue making money.[xii] Trudeau explains that when Napoleon Hill wrote *Think and Grow Rich,* Henry Ford did everything in his power to keep the book from getting out into the general market. According to Trudeau, the very rich wanted this principle to be kept a "secret." It was their own "genie in a bottle" and from what Trudeau says, the rich really know how to work this principle consistently. The billionaires in this world have all learned this from each other and manipulated it to gain more wealth. Trudeau also states that the wealthy believe they were born to be wealthy, so sharing this principle with the lower classes would not matter because they are not entitled to wealth. (He made this as a general statement.)[xiii]

It seems that secret societies have been making application of "as a man thinketh" from Psalms 23:7 without knowing the God who wrote that scripture.[xiv] That sounds like faith to me. They have faith in a principle, but not in a person. Does this concept make you feel uncomfortable? Does it seem wrong to believe in good things happening to you or wishing for your heart's desires without "delighting in the Lord" (Psalm 37:4)? This was one of the problems the church (in general) had with the book *The Secret.* The next chapter suggests other conflicts.

I believe with the rapidly spreading teachings on quantum physics, that perhaps "the secret" was destined to "get out" and then those who have guarded this for decades decided to be involved in the release of this information. I pray the next few chapters will bring some understanding of the laws of the universe and how I believe God wants us to understand and apply them.

CHAPTER 3
THE CHRISTIAN CHURCH'S
CONFLICTS WITH *THE SECRET'S*
CONTENT

T he "name it and claim it" theology and practices from the "Word of Faith" movement experienced a peak in the early nineties. I remember being a young, on-fire Christian listening to popular tel-evangelists make some questionable claims. Some would attempt to sell pieces of "anointed fabric" that, like Paul's anointing, were guaranteed to bring healing or miracles. Others would promise a thousand fold return on a financial investment. These claims seemed ludicrous in the natural, but my faith was challenged. I used to think, "Well this must be real because millions of people watch this guy. Maybe I have the problem." Eventually, many of these "ministers" were indicted for fraud. After the exposure of corruption and deception by the TV evangelists who promoted this theology, many Christians were left with a bad taste in their mouths for the principles espoused.

Instead of seeing the whole picture of true abundance and prosperity that the Bible suggests, the immature application of faith suggests that by simply asking for cars, money, and furs, they will appear. These televangelists took advantage of this "magical" principle by promising wealth to those who sent money, while they were exploiting the wealth deceptively. As a knee-jerk reaction, many people "threw the baby out with the bath water" and, in their hearts, vowed that wealth was evil. There is much debate theologically on wealth and though that is not the purpose of this book, scripture points to the **condition of the heart** as a central issue in regard to wealth.

No thing, in and of itself, is inherently evil, only what we do with it. Wealth is a necessary tool for the spread of the gospel and ministry across the world and it can also be an idol and bondage. It depends on how it is viewed by the person. Is it an idol? Does it require corruption to maintain or produce? Proverbs and other scripture repeatedly tell us that poverty is undesirable and a curse. But in scripture, wealth is also discussed with great caution. Again, my point is not to debate theology, but to share my observations.

I believe when *The Secret* emerged, especially in a mulimedia format, it sounded much like the "name it claim it" gospel that didn't include a relationship with Jesus. This was my initial response to seeing the video. I thought, "This is just about greed and material-ism."

I believe the principles of quantum physics and the Bible reciprocally support each other and that is the purpose of this book. However, every truth can be mistaught and abused. Religionists and theologians love to extol their intellectual arguments to dismantle truth. I am not defending the book, *The Secret*, only again pointing out the Christian church's ten-dency to "throw the baby out with the bath water."

I believe the bottom line is God wants us to live and prosper, however that is defined. The Bible supports this and depicts poverty as a curse.

The problem is always a heart issue, not a wealth issue.

The Kingdom of God requires money to expand. Running from wealth for fear of corruption will probably ensure you stay poor. Looking to God for a pure heart about wealth is a far better solution than poverty. 1 John 2:15 (New International Version) says:

[15] Do not love the world or anything in the world. If anyone loves the world, love for the Father is not in them. [16] For everything in the world—the lust of the flesh, the lust of the eyes, and the pride of life—comes not from the Father but from the world. [17]The world and its desires pass away, but whoever does the will of God lives forever.

God does not want us to lust after worldly things, but, once again, factions of the church want to "throw the baby out with the bath wa-ter." Wealth is about stewardship of God's finances for the Kingdom, not about hedonistic pleasures or seeking happiness in material possessions. Perhaps having wealth lends itself to greater temptation but poverty is definitely seen as a curse.

Having established this thought, the problem many had with *The Secret* is similar to the "name it and claim it" theology. Because the author was not a professing Christian, it was inclusive to the whole world, not just Christian believers. It does not state the existence of a God who is the creator, but talks about an anonymous universe that is for us only because we believe it is for us, when in fact it is neutral. As you will see later, I believe God created the laws of attraction to govern the universe, but he gave us the outline of these laws in the Bible. Scripture tells us how the universe is governed, if we will listen and follow. This was not "metaphysical." It was written plainly, long before the "self-help gurus" set foot on the earth. We do not look to the universe, we look to God. The principles of the *The Secret* are predominantly Biblical; it is the lack of professing God as creator of the universe that can create disharmony with our spirit.

The Secret suggests our lives are blank slates and that we can potentially create multiple possibilities for ourselves. Christianity portrays a sovereign God who:

- Knew you from your mother's womb...
  Psalm 139:13 (Amplified Bible): "For You did form my inward parts; You did knit me together in my mother's womb."
  Jeremiah 1:4-5 (New American Standard Bible): "The word of the LORD came to me saying, [5]Before I formed you in the womb I knew you, And before you were born I consecrated you; I have appointed you a prophet to the nations."
- Knows the number of hairs on your head...
  Luke 12:7 (NIV): "Indeed, the very hairs of your head are all numbered. Don't be afraid; you are worth more than many sparrows."

- Has a destiny for you...

> Ephesians 1:5: "He predestined us for adoption
> to sonship through Jesus Christ, in accordance with
> his pleasure and Will."
>
> Jeremiah 29:11-13: " [11] For I know the plans
> I have for you,' declares the LORD, 'plans to
> prosper you and not to harm you, plans to give
> you hope and a future. [12] Then you will call on me
> and come and pray to me, and I will listen to you.
> [13] You will seek me and find me when you seek me
> with all your heart.' " (A specific word to Israel, but
> showing God was involved in destiny.)
>
> Romans 8:28-31: " [28] And we know that in all things
> God works for the good of those who love him, who
> have been called according to his purpose. [29] For
> those God foreknew he also predestined to be
> conformed to the image of his Son, that he might
> be the firstborn among many brothers and sisters.
> [30] And those he predestined, he also called; those
> he called, he also justified; those he justified, he
> also glorified. [31] What, then, shall we say in re-
> sponse to these things? If God is for us, who can be
> against us?"

Another reason I believe *The Secret* was rejected by the church was because many people interpreted the movie as being solely materialistic. The central theme of the gospel is that we "lose our life to find it" (Matthew 10:39), that we "throw aside all weights" (which could include material things) and "run the race" (Hebrews 12:1), and "run [your race] that you may lay hold [of the prize] and make it yours"(1 Corinthians 9:24). It says in Luke 9:23 (Expanded Bible) that we should "deny himself [disown himself, forget, lose sight of himself and his own interests, refuse and give up himself] and take up his cross daily and follow Me" and again in 1 Corinthians 15:31, that we should "die daily" to ourselves.

25

We are suppose to live our lives with the mindset that the body is not our home and at odds with being with the Lord (2 Corinthians 5:6) and with the goal to hear Him say in Heaven, "well done my good and faithful servant" (Luke 19:17).

These scriptures imply that we should not seek comfort or things for ourselves, but that everything is related to the gospel and making disciples. *The Secret* seemingly comes across with the message that having everything we think we want will make us happy. The Bible suggests true "happiness," which we would translate to "peace and joy," comes from surrendering our will to Jesus and seeking a relationship with Him. We must forsake all else for Him to become our primary, authentic source of happiness.

I would also suggest that one of the issues many Christians may have had with *The Secret* was the thought, "surely it can't be this easy." There is always this underlying voice of our flesh that we have to work hard for everything, even our relationship with the Lord. We easily miss the grace part of the gospel because religion and the secular worldview constantly remind us that performance is necessary. The people who are successful in law of attraction work have a simple faith that this principle is the governing structure of the universe that they simply have to apply. They divorce it from an existing God who governs the law of attraction. Ultimately, they separate the principle from any kind of relationship.

Many of those in the body of Christ have significant father wounds from our childhood. The belief that the God of the universe loves us and wants to give us the desires of our heart triggers painful, subconscious memories of an earthly father who does not fit the description of a loving God. It offends us to think that the universe is like a vending machine and yet the law of attraction does suggest a slightly more complex version of this.

The Secret book does elaborate more than the movie. It talks about having "stuff," but ultimately, it points to an inner peace as the source of true happiness. The thought that having everything we want seems hedonistic to a Christian, but then many Christians spend their lives scrambling just to survive, never achieving a state of peace and joy because they have not been able to experience the scriptures just mentioned. There are many reasons why they cannot achieve a state of peace and joy; it is not a simple task. As you continue to read, I believe you will be enlightened about exactly where the law of attraction fits into God's big scheme of things and how to use it in your life in a way that aligns with God's Heart and His Word.

At the end of his life, Billy Graham made the statement that he wished he had spent "more time alone with God and less time doing ministry." Wow! Can you imagine being the single most successful minister of this century, a household name, not having any need for material things, having successful, fulfilling relationships, and making this statement? This reveals a deep truth that our greatest place of peace and joy comes from intimacy with the Holy Spirit.

The Law of Grace and the Science of Chaos

While *The Secret* presents quantum physics truths, it does not account for the law of grace and mercy. We know that the law of gravity applies to humans most of the time. Rarely can someone jump off a five-story building and not splat onto the ground. (I don't suggest you try it.) Peter walked on water, but I have yet to meet someone who has truly done this successfully (Matthew 14:22-23). The rules of aerodynamics trump the law of gravity so airplanes and birds can fly. Chapter five will discuss law hierarchy in more in depth. *The Secret* does not suggest there are hierarchies, whereas the Bible does. *The Secret* does not make place for a supernatural, loving God who is involved in the affairs of men, but the Bible does.

There is a principle in meteorology called the "science of chaos." This principle suggests that the laws of weather are so intertwined, they cannot truly be accurately predicted. It refers to the "butterfly effect" as an example of this. The butterfly effect explains how the flight pattern of a butterfly in Rio de Janeiro could affect the weather in New York City. The whole world affects every other part so intricately that meteorologists can never be 100% accurate in forecasting weather because they cannot factor in all of the variables accurately (quantum physics includes this in the law of entanglement).[xv] I believe God's operations in the world are similar to this law. His complexity is far beyond our understanding and sometimes He chooses to override natural laws, like He did when Peter stepped out of the boat. *The Secret* does not allow for this idea that a supernatural God might trump the law of attraction, but testimonies confirm otherwise. *The Secret* might agree that your faith (like Peter's) could cause you to override natural laws, but that theory would not explain why Shadrach, Meshach, and Abednego did not burn when cast into the fiery furnace. The hand of God can and does transcend all other laws. He is always involved and perhaps, if we were smarter, we would discover all of His actions are governed by laws. Supernatural stories throughout history suggest He does not always stay within the guidelines He set forth for the universe to operate. It is man's nature to try to order his own world by creating rules and structures to make himself feel safe. *The Secret* gives pat formulas for all operations. Exceptions suggest there are more complex rules than just these. *The Secret* would suggest that if something doesn't manifest, you either didn't really want it or you were conflicted in your subconscious. This makes exceptions easy to explain. Supernatural occurrences might suggest the law of attraction is not including God's direct intervention or that the science of chaos might be involved. I would posit that the prayers of other people are a key factor in the science of chaos. We are all connected.

So while the principle of the law of attraction is true in how we live our lives (as will be discussed in the next chapters), the neat package suggested by *The Secret* negates a personal God who may sovereignly move, undeservedly, and in mysterious ways while displaying His glory in a person's life. He may have created the law of attraction to govern the universe, but He still remains and wants us to remember He is God over all of His creation and is personally involved. Everything is not always left entirely to some computer-like mechanistic process.

As I have listened to tapes and read law of attraction books, I have become intrigued by this concept that we create our own destiny. As you will read, I support this idea with scripture and spiritual laws. However, what makes my life so incredible is I have a personal relationship with a real and living God. His presence has no words to compare and is unlike any other sensation. The connection I feel with the Holy Spirit at any given moment (when I pay attention) makes all of the stuff and success of this world pale in comparison. The law of attraction cannot counterfeit this and it truly is ours for the asking. We have to seek and desire it like everything else. We have to believe it is real, although the Holy Spirit apprehends many who don't believe in Him prior to this apprehension. So perhaps we, as Christians, can have the best of both worlds: a powerful relationship with Jesus Christ, the Father, and the Holy Spirit *and* the understanding of how to manifest a kingdom destiny of good fruit using principles of attraction.

So, as I proposed earlier, what if God created the law of attraction to essentially govern the universe? Everything He does has an order to it. We can observe this in nature and science at any given moment. What if the theory of the law of attraction is not a different, New Age, or metaphysical theory? What if it is completely supported by Scripture? What if God's design was for the universe to fundamentally run by the principles of quantum physics? What if much of what we are taught in Scripture is, in fact, quantum physics principles? A few key principles of quantum physics can be understood in the following statements:

1. You attract what you think and believe — the law of attraction
2. You get what you give/reap what you sow — the law of reciprocity
3. You create your own world with what you believe and whatever you focus attention on/give energy to grow and/or manifest — the law of expansion
4. Waves intensify when the are in unison with other sources — the law of entrainment

In the next chapters, each of these four laws will be addressed with scripture alongside the scientific understanding of each principle.

CHAPTER 4
SCRIPTURES SUPPORTING THE
LAW OF ATTRACTION

Before exploring further, it is vital to grasp an important concept called the "Iceberg Principle." You and I are like icebergs. What does that mean? Brain science research seems to concur that there are anywhere from 85 billion to 2.5 trillion neurons firing in the brain every second, but we are only conscious of less than 5% of this activity.[xvi] The other 95% is occurring without our conscious awareness, although our subconscious (the iceberg under the water) is picking up on everything.[xvii] We are truly supercomputers analyzing billions of bytes of data daily, yet only consciously aware of a small part. Our life is being run by our subconscious. We don't realize this because we don't know what we don't know.

Proverbs 23:7 (NIV):
As a man thinks in his heart, so is he...

Romans 12:2:
Do not conform to the pattern of this world, but be transformed
by the renewing of your mind...

Taco Bell (a Pepsi corporation) typically spends half a million dollars for a thirty second TV commercial during the Super Bowl. Wow! They have to sell a substantial amount of tacos to pay for that commercial and justify it as a rational investment. Their research into the effect that commercials have in "programming" the millions watching the Super Bowl must have shown it would pay off. The bottom line is we are being programmed by everything we hear, see, touch, smell, think, and speak. Because of the iceberg effect, you may not be aware as to why you suddenly want Taco Bell a couple days after you saw that Super Bowl commercial. Your subconscious mind watched that commercial, gave it meaning and value, and left an imprint.

The experiments of Dr. Emoto I discussed previously show the effects of thinking on molecules of water. Remember he conducted different experiments: some with music, some with words spoken, and some with words written (intention/thought).

Using science, Emoto confirmed that vibrations from the intentions, music, or words altered the molecular structure of the water samples. Remember, everything has vibration and 60% of the human body is made up of water. When we watched that Taco Bell commercial, the vibrations and waves were imprinted in our iceberg, giving it meaning. We do this hundreds of times a day.

As I have become more aware of frequency waves and programming, I have noticed how we are programmed by our environment, media, movies, music, and culture. Hollywood's blatant deception in their veiled entertainment has become more obvious with each movie produced. While many plot lines may seem ludicrous or sci-fi, they actually involve real technology and strategy. One movie that comes to mind is the comedy "Josie and the Pussycats" which was released in 2001. In the movie, Josie and her girls are discovered and promoted as the next new pop group. The musical group is a cover-up for a military mind control operation that is testing whether or not people can be widely controlled starting by tricking the general population to buy into specific trends. We know music and frequencies are powerful tools to program. The frequencies program the water in your body, which can take root in your mind.

When Paul was talking about taking thoughts captive and making them obedient to Christ in 2 Corinthians 10:5, he was acknowledging how we are simultaneously unaware of and influenced by our surroundings. This scripture is warning us that because we can be subconsciously imprinted by our world, we must practice "mindfulness" by constantly make our thoughts align with truth.

Medical science has confirmed that more than 80% of disease is rooted in problems in subconscious belief systems. If we are only conscious of about 5% of the 60,000+ thoughts we think every day, then our life is guided by our subconscious. (I will use subconscious synonymously with the word "heart.") This aligns with the law of attraction. If our past is wrought with trauma, abuse, and pain, our subconscious belief systems about ourselves will be dominated by self- hate, low self-esteem, bitterness, resentment, blame, self-pity, jealousy, anger, fear, and other forms of these emotions. If "like attracts like," we will become what we think.

Why is it so hard for many people to truly believe that if they delight themselves in the Lord, He will give them good things? I believe the answer lies in a deep, subconscious mistrust in their relationship with the Lord. I have been connected to various ministries over the years that were focused on healing the "father wound" — a deep wound left from an unhealthy relationship with a natural father that causes a struggle in real intimacy and trust in Father God. Those who have received healing in this area can attest to the change before and after in their connection to a loving Father God. The subconscious block of distrust cannot be easily overridden by a simple will to connect. Safety is felt, not willed, and the subconscious is more powerful than the conscious desire to believe God is good

Many Christians will say they believe the Bible is true, but if we are icebergs and our subconscious is more powerful than our conscious, then what we believe in our conscious mind is overruled by our actual beliefs. We do not know many of these subconscious beliefs, all of which were influenced or created by our programming experiences in life.

Matthew 9:29 (AMP) says:
Then he touched their eyes, saying, "According to your faith, (and trust and reliance on the power in me) be it done to you."

Matthew 21:21 says:
And Jesus answered them, "Truly I say to you, if you have faith (a firm relying trust) and do not doubt, you will not only do what has

been done to the fig tree, but even if you say to this mountain, be taken up and cast into the sea, it will be done."

Apparently God feels this bears repeating. Mark 11:23 says:
Truly I say to you, whoever says to this mountain, be lifted up and thrown into the sea and does not doubt at all in his heart, but believes that what he says will take place, it will be done for him.

The word "believe" is found in the Book of John 83 times (in the Amplified Bible).

John 14:1 says:
Do not let your hearts be troubled, distressed, agitated. You believe (in and adhere to and trust in and rely) on God; believe (in and adhere to and trust in and rely) also on Me.

Matthew 8:13 says:
Then to the centurion Jesus said, "Go; it shall be done for you as you have believed. And the servant boy was restored to health at that very moment."

Often I have seen the church limit their definition of the word "believe" to the concept of the gospel only—believing Jesus is God and died for our sins—but Jesus is talking about so much more of what his sacrifice actually means for us.

The word "believe" consistently contains these three meanings: rely, trust, and adhere to. We call this "faith" and it has implications on our thought-life in every conscious and subconscious detail. Jesus repeatedly links belief with the impossible. He connects faith with seeing those things manifest. He says many times that in order for it to manifest, we must not doubt. James 1:5-8 (NIV) says:

5If any of you lacks wisdom, you should ask God, who gives generously to all without finding fault, and it will be given to you. 6But when you ask, you must believe and not doubt, because the one who doubts is like a wave of the sea, blown and tossed by the wind. [7]That person should not expect to receive anything from the Lord. [8]Such a person is double-minded and unstable in all they do.

Whatever we have belief in/have faith for/focus our attention on, we empower and it grows. Jesus repeatedly told us to have faith, to believe. Faith is the energy that empowers the vibration, high or low. He encourages us to have faith for good things like provision and abundance, His love for us, and supernatural outpourings of His power. Like attracts like. James clearly states that if we doubt God gives generously and does it without finding fault (like we think we have to earn it), then we walk in doubt and should not expect to receive it. In other words, it isn't because God doesn't want us to have what we desire. He says clearly in Psalms 37:4 (NASB): "Delight yourself in the Lord and He will give you the desires of your heart." The problem is we doubt His goodness and we don't rely, trust, or adhere to this attribute about Him. Doubt and fear do not vibrate high and don't attract good things. When we sow faith, we move mountains, when we sow doubt, we don't. Fear, worry, and doubt vibrate very low and attract like things.

I was always puzzled by Matthew 25:29 (AMP). It reads:

For to everyone who has will more be given, and he will be furnished richly so that he will have an abundance; but from the one who does not have, even what he does have will be taken away.

I have never really heard a satisfactory explanation of what Jesus was talking about in this scripture. What if Jesus is referring to the law of attraction? Those who "have" have understood to ask, seek, and knock while keeping a high vibration to continue attracting more good things. Those who are in lack have kept a low vibration, lacking faith and living in a constant state of worry. If they continue to doubt and vibrate low, they will continue to lose what they do have. God is no respecter of persons. He gives us the guideline to live a life of peace and joy if we will choose to follow the blueprint. Pause and review your life for a few minutes applying this concept. See if you can identify any patterns where your beliefs about things, yourself, others, God, and/or the universe have been reinforced in your experience. Now look at other peoples' lives. Do they all share the same reinforced negative experiences? When our experiences are not universally true, then it's highly possible we made them up and are attracting what we believe.

Matthew 6:25-31 (NIV) says:

Don't worry about food, clothes, drink etc. [26]Look at the birds of the air, they neither sow nor reap nor gather into barns, and yet your heavenly father keeps feeding them. Are you not worth much more than they? [27]And who of you by working and being anxious can add one unit of measure to his stature or to the span of his life? [28]Consider the lilies of the field and learn thoroughly how they grow; they neither toil nor spin. [29]Yet I tell you, even Solomon in all of his magnificence was not arrayed like one of these. [30]But if God so clothes the grass of the field, which today is alive and green and tomorrow is tossed into the furnace, will He not much more surely clothe you, you of little faith? [31]Therefore, do not worry... your heavenly Father knows well that you need them all.

Jesus was making this statement about the character of God to the masses, not just his followers. He clearly says that God (not the universe) knows your needs. He also makes it clear that being a Christian believer is not a prerequisite for Him meeting your needs.

There are spiritual and scriptural reasons why people still go without and many places across the globe where poverty exists as a curse. This is evil at work in the world. Many of the people in these poverty-stricken cultures worship and serve gods who do not have their best interest in mind (and they do not know a loving Father God). Jesus is talking to those who believe they serve a loving and providing Father God. This scripture illustrates the principle of getting what we believe, think, or expect. It illustrates the concept that God is for us and will take care of our needs. He is encouraging us to operate in faith in order to have the vibration we need to attract good things. God wants to do this but we must align with His truth.

Jesus says in Matthew 6:33:

But seek first of all **His kingdom** (New King James says, "the kingdom of God") and his righteousness and then all these things taken together will be given you.

"All these things" is a reference to food, clothes, drink, and other provision named previously in Matthew 6:25-31. Jesus is saying if we will seek the kingdom of God first, rather than spending our time and energy worrying about meeting needs ourselves, all of our needs will be met. So, what is "the kingdom of God"? One of the most impactful revelations I've had came from a bible study I attended for several years.[xviii] The definition of "the kingdom of God" is given in Romans 14:17-18 (AMP):

[After all] the kingdom of God is not a matter of [getting the] food and drink [one likes], but instead it is righteousness (that state which makes a person acceptable to God) and [heart] peace and joy in the Holy Spirit.

So if we seek these three things:

1. **righteousness** (Jesus is our righteousness because ours is as "filthy rags" [Isaiah 64:6])
2. **peace** (absence of fear, trust in Him)
3. **joy** (relationship with Jesus)

Then, we will have all that we need ("all these things"). If we seek after our needs, then we are operating in doubt and worry (and are double-minded according to James). Peace and joy vibrate high. Worry vibrates low. What we think, and the emotional state we are in, creates a vibration/frequency that attracts things in our lives accordingly. When we vibrate high, we have man's favor while attracting good things, but ultimately, we please God (because that is faith).

Many years ago, when I was pregnant with my eldest daughter, I worked in ministry and made very little money (but I loved my job). I woke up one morning and simply had the thought, "I have outgrown my undergarments and could really use some new ones." I continued getting ready for the day and headed off to work without a second thought on this. When I arrived to work that same day, I checked the donation drop box like usual as this was one of my job duties. To my surprise, there was a bag full of brand new bras from a nice department store that were exactly the size I needed. That morning, I had sent up a minor request and because I was serving God's kingdom, the request was answered. This type of situation has happened to me countless times over the years, sometimes with fulfillment happening in the same day, like in this instance. Back then, I didn't understand the principles of quantum physics, but I was operating in the biblical criteria for manifestation. It's not a formula, but a principle that God created. Like attracts like.

Did you know that in the advent of brain science, it was discovered the brain is wired for peace and joy? Dr. Alan Schore has done extensive research on the physiology of the brain and written on this topic.[xix] E. James Wilder and his colleagues simplified these very complicated books to explain that **God wired our brains for peace and joy**.[xx] Everything we do is motivated by our brain's attempts to return to a state of peace or joy. For example, babies need secure attachments in order to bring them from a state of distress back to peace and joy. This is crucial in the brain's ability to later on be able to return to states of peace and joy. Addictions, compulsions, everything we do, is motivated by a drive to return to this state. Freud called this "the pleasure principle." It has often been misunderstood by critics to say that Freud believed we are driven by pleasure as in how we define "hedonism," but really we are driven by our belief systems. If worry allows us to feel in control, then that brings a degree of peace to our mind. But fear and worry lead to attracting low vibration or negative things. Authentic joy and peace that come from trusting in the Lord for everything vibrate high and attract high vibrations or good things. Trust is a scary thing because it must be rooted in a deep knowing that we are loved. 1 John 5:14-15 (NIV) says:

> [14] This is the confidence we have in approaching God: that if we ask anything according to His will, He hears us. [15] And if we know that He hears us—whatever we ask—we know that we have what we asked of Him.

We know God wants to give us the desires of our heart. (This is His will). If we are delighting in Him, then we can believe our heart's desires will align with what is good for our lives (at least in general). And if we don't doubt (James 1), then our desires will manifest. This defines exactly what the law of attraction says in principle. The question becomes, "What do we truly desire?" The challenge is more about how to actually execute living a life of peace and joy, which I will address in subsequent chapters.

Another revelation I had while attending the same bible study was regarding what the Bible actually defines as God's will. In Ephesians 5:17-20, Paul writes:

> [7]Therefore do not be foolish, but understand what the Lord's will is. [18] Do not get drunk on wine, which leads to debauchery. Instead, be filled with the Spirit, [19] speaking to one another with psalms, hymns, and songs from the Spirit. Sing and make music from your heart to the Lord, [20] always giving thanks to God the Father for everything, in the name of our Lord Jesus Christ.

God's will is for us to:
1. Not seek after hedonistic pleasures (debauchery)
2. Be filled with the Spirit instead of the world (seek to sow to the spirit and not the flesh)

3. Edify and encourage each other; affirm and do not criticize each other
4. Worship the Lord in our heart
5. Live in a state of gratitude to the Lord

All of these things are high vibration states of existence. God's will is that we stay in a state of peace and joy, which is the Kingdom of God. This is different from destiny, callings, anointing, and spheres of influence.

So how do we do this? It seems like an impossible task. The world is full of pain, evil, stress, sickness, hunger, and many other negative things. We are bombarded every day with negative events that send us the message that life is cruel and the universe is against us. We are continually fed the idea that the way to solve the world's problems is to worry. Joy and peace seem like they can only belong to heartless, cold, and self-centered human beings who don't care about the rest of the world. Philippians 4:6-8 gives us the simple answer:

> [6]Do not be anxious about anything, but in every situation, by prayer and petition, with thanksgiving, present your requests to God. [7]And the peace of God, which transcends all understanding, will guard your hearts and your minds in Christ Jesus. [8]Finally, brothers and sisters, whatever is true, whatever is noble, whatever is right, whatever is pure, whatever is lovely, whatever is admirable—if anything is excellent or praiseworthy—think about such things.

Paul is saying something incredible. He is telling us not to think about anything negative. He is saying God wants us to focus only on positive things, period. We would call that having a "Pollyanna" outlook. But in effect, the law of attraction principles and the scriptures just discussed are saying this very thing. Whatever we focus on is what we empower. It impacts our body, soul, and spirit. Staying at a place of peace and joy requires us to be in control of our thoughts and deliberately choose to focus on positive things. Remember Dr. Emoto's water experiments.

Throughout my years of observation, I have found that few people experience true peace. The mantra of most people today, in our busy and complex world, is: "There is much to worry about." What many people don't realize is that worry is a learned trait. As children, we watch our parents worry and therefore model their behavior as we mature, believing that being an adult requires us to apply anxiety and fear to our problems. Can you find patterns of anxiety or worry in your own life?

Peace requires a deliberate seeking out. Many people attribute peace to irresponsibility (believing as I did that responsible people must worry) and boredom. Some people feel useless when they are at peace because they attribute busyness to self-worth. The content of this book will (hopefully) convince you that peace is the most powerful state you can achieve for both your own life and for the purpose of God's Kingdom. Before beginning the next chapter, pause for a moment and think of ways you can replace your habit of worry with a mindset of peace.

CHAPTER 5
SCRIPTURES SUPPORTING
THE LAW OF RECIPROCITY

The second basic principle of quantum physics is called the law of reciprocity. In basic terms, we get what we give. We give love and get love in return. We give greed and selfishness, we get greed and selfishness in return. This is the law of reciprocity. In energy terms, whatever energy gets sent out (thoughts, intentions, emotions, etc.) will come back to us. The vibration sent out will bounce back.

The word "karma" has become a household word. It is used in Hindu and other religious philosophies in reference to life's lessons which determine future lives.[xxi] Since Christianity does not embrace reincarnation, the household understanding of karma is the idea of cause and effect. It means that whatever we do sets action in motion and there is a consequence to us. A common application of karma would be if you help an old lady walk across the street, something good will happen to you. In the Bible, we see the concept of sowing and reaping. Galatians 6:7-10 says:

> [7]Do not be deceived: God cannot be mocked. A man reaps what he sows. [8]Whoever sows to please their flesh, from the flesh will reap destruction; whoever sows to please the Spirit, from the Spirit will reap eternal life. [9]Let us not become weary in doing good, for at the proper time we will reap a harvest if we do not give up. [10]Therefore, as we have opportunity, let us do good to all people, especially to those who belong to the family of believers.

This passage is saying a great deal about the spiritual principles that govern the universe and what most people think of as "karma." The law of attraction is all about sowing and reaping because "like attracts like." There are many scriptures where this principle is even further detailed. In Matthew 13, Jesus gives the parable of the farmer sowing seeds, the parable of the mustard seed and yeast:

> [23] But the seed falling on good soil refers to someone who hears the word and understands it. This is the one who produces a crop, yielding a hundred, sixty or thirty times what was sown. [31] He told them another parable: "The kingdom of heaven is like a mustard seed, which a man took and planted in his field. [32] Though it is the smallest of all seeds, yet when it grows, it is the largest of garden plants and becomes a tree, so that the birds come and perch in its branches." [33] He told them still another parable: "The kingdom of heaven is like yeast that a woman took and mixed into about sixty pounds of flour until it worked all through the dough."

Jesus gives metaphors of the concept of multiplication. When we sow, what we reap is much greater.

Luke 6:38 (EXB) says:
Give, and you will receive [it will be given to you]. You will be given much (...a good Luke 6:38 measure...). Pressed down [Compacted], shaken together, and running over, it will spill into your lap [the image is of grain overflowing its container]. The way you give to [standard/measure you use with] others is the way God will give to [standard/measure God will use with] you.

In this verse, Jesus says that what you reap will be expanded from what you sow. Perhaps Jesus is talking about the manner in which you give or, in other words, the state of your heart/the intention behind why you give. The return is multiplied based upon the intention when you sow. The law of attraction focuses on your thoughts or intentions. So, you could give with bad intention (reluctantly) and not have the same result as giving with good intention. We can give in order to get and the principle still works, but I believe the greater multiplication happens when we give to give because the vibration is higher. When we give out of love, we attract a greater return than giving out of law.

2 Corinthians 9:7 (AMP) says:
Let each one [give] as he has made up his own mind and purposed in his heart, not reluctantly or sorrowfully or under compulsion, for God loves (He takes pleasure in, prizes above other things, and is unwilling to abandon or to do without) a cheerful (joyous, "prompt to do it") giver [whose heart is in his giving].

Malachi 3:10 says:
"Bring all the tithes (the whole tenth of your income) into the storehouse, that there may be food in my house, and prove Me now by it," says the Lord of hosts, "if I will not open the windows of heaven for you and pour you out a blessing, that there shall not be room enough to receive it."

This principle applies to giving in general, not just money. The point is about having the intention to bless God, others, and God's kingdom and to do good. Remember that the harvest is always a multiplication of what was planted. The law of reciprocity says we should repay kindness for kindness or pay it forward. It says if we practice love and kindness (both high vibrations), we will attract the same. The law of sowing and reaping, according to the Bible, is better. It says that what we give will be supernaturally multiplied when it is returned to us. This is about expansion. When we give with the intention of blessing God or the kingdom of God, we, in effect, sow a mustard seed and the return is great.

I love this example of giving being multiplied: Mary Elaine held a Bible study in her home. Her family was going through a tough time financially, but God allowed them to maintain their nice home. There were days when they didn't have enough food. Strangers came to the meetings in her home all the time. One day, someone told her that God wanted them to give her some money and held out a wad of cash. Mary Elaine stuffed it in her pocket without counting it. She was thinking about the food they could buy for their five kids. A little while later, during the Bible study, the Lord told Mary Elaine to give the wad of cash to a visiting missionary couple. Still, without counting the money, she obediently handed them the cash **with great joy**. Not long after that, someone pulled up into her driveway with an SUV loaded from top to bottom with food. She determined it was much more than the cash she had given away. In the same day, Mary Elaine demonstrated this principle by receiving, then giving, and receiving even more. Over the years, I have heard countless examples of these types of stories. You can never out-give God. I have seen and experienced this firsthand as have most of my friends and fellow believers.

Have you ever experienced a giving miracle? Have you given sacrificially and seen it multiply back or have any of your friends had this happen to them?

The Law of Bitter Root Judgments

The law of bitter root judgments is a subcategory of the law of sowing and reaping. This is one of the fundamental principles developed by John and Paula Sandford of Elijah House International decades ago and has been implemented in prayer ministry for many thousands of people all over the world. I have found it to consistently operate in people's lives according to its principles. The principle is founded on Matthew 7:1-5 which says:

> [1]Do not judge and criticize and condemn others, so that you may not be judged and criticized and condemned yourselves. [2]For just as you judge and criticize and condemn others, you will be judged and criticized and condemned, and in accordance with the measure you [use to] deal out to others, it will be dealt out again to you. [3]Why do you stare at the very small particle that is in your brother's eye but do not become aware of and consider

the beam of timber that is in your own eye? [4]Or how can you say to your brother, "Let me get the tiny particle out of your eye, when there is the beam of timber in your own eye." [5]You hypocrite, first get the beam of timber out of your own eye, and then you will see clearly to take the tiny particle out of your brother's eye.

John Sandford developed the principle of "bitter root judgments." The law of bitter root judgments says that however you judge another person in your heart, that judgement will be sent back to you and manifest in your own life. It may manifest by you directly experiencing the thing you judged or it may manifest in your spouse (because you are one with your spouse). He develops this principle using Matthew 7:1-5, Galatians 6:7, and the command to honor our father and mother in Exodus 20:12. Matthew 7:18 states that a good tree cannot bear bad fruit and vice versa. So, seeds of judgment will produce bad trees in our life and we identify the bad trees by acknowledging the bad fruit.

If we are aware enough to identify the bad fruit, we can track the fruit back to the bad trees and roots of judgment. Roots of bitterness defile others, as described in Hebrews 12:15. This principle has been confirmed and used in ministry and inner healing for decades from training models such as Elijah House, Restoring the Foundations, and Freedom and Fullness. Many thousands of people will verify the areas in their life where they have judged others, especially their parents, have manifested the same experiences in their own life. Or they married someone who manifested the things they judged. "As a man thinks in his heart" means that when we maintain constant thoughts that are judgmental or critical towards someone, we send negative intentions into the universe. These are low vibration thoughts that will come back to us. **These judgments cause us to hold onto bitterness or resentment which become trapped and cause these persistent thoughts.**

When we sow criticism, we reap criticism. When we sow bitterness, we reap bitterness. When we curse someone, even in our hearts or thoughts, we send negative vibrations into the universe that come back to us. Bless and we are blessed; curse and we are cursed; forgive and we are forgiven; judge and we are judged; love and we are loved. With God, our intentions are not just reciprocated, but multiplied back to us. So if our intentions are positive, they are multiplied positively and if they are negative, they are multiplied negatively.

Let me add a disclaimer that not everything bad that happens is because you made a judgment when you were a child. There are other causes in the universe for adversity, I am just focusing on bitter root judgments.

I could give many examples of this principle manifesting in my personal life. I can remember God illustrating this to me one day when my husband lost his keys. (He tended to misplace them every day.) I remember thinking, "How can you do this every day? Why don't you just put them in the same place everyday so you know where they are?" (which he later did). I was more irritated by the anger he displayed (towards himself) which triggered some of my own issues with anger and I definitely judged him in my heart. That same day, I misplaced my keys in the house (which I hardly ever do). I remember laughing out loud as I realized God was illustrating this principle to me clearly. I have spent the better part of twenty-five years making a concerted effort to become aware of my thoughts when I am judging. I make a point at the beginning or end of each day to review my thoughts and see whom I have judged, forgive them, and repent. This principle is also illustrated in Romans 2:2:

> Therefore, you have no excuse or defense or justification, O man, whoever you are who judges and condemns another. For in posing as judge and passing sentence on another, you condemn yourself, because you who judge are habitually practicing the very same things [that you censure and denounce].

I have noticed in my own marriage and in the marriages of people I know, that repeated arguments and conflicts almost always point back to childhood judgments both parties made of their parents (or siblings). They are then repeating the pattern of reaping and re-sowing the same judgments with the thoughts, "You are just like my _____ who also did _____ or was _____." This reciprocal reaping also illustrates the principle of "defilement." Hebrews 12:15 (NIV) says:

> See to it that no one falls short of the grace of God and that no bitter root grows up to cause trouble and defile many.

What this means is if we have judged someone in some area and carry that around, there is a pressure for other people to treat us in the manner we reap from the judgment. I have often seen this principle in action.

From a psychological perspective, the area we have judged contains "unfinished business." This is popular concept was developed by Fritz Perlz in Gestalt therapy. Unfinished business means we are still holding beliefs, bitterness, resentment, pride, and deep hurt from the person we judged. Gestalt therapy says we will surround ourselves with people who "finish our business" in the subconscious because we couldn't finish it with the original person. So if our dad abandoned us, we will continue to encounter men who will abandon us as we subconsciously try to fix our abandonment issues from an earlier age. Vibrationally, we believe men will abandon us and that belief is deeply programmed in our subconscious, causing us to continue attracting to what we believe.

While Gestalt psychologists call this "unfinished business," other authorities label it as "trauma bonding" or "trauma reenactment." These terms are just a psychological explanation for the spiritual principle of bitter root judgments (also known in quantum physics as the law of attraction and the law of reciprocity). The same outcome/bad fruit can be explained spiritually, psychologically, scientifically, and vibrationally.

One example of this was a client of mine who grew up with a younger brother who had schizophrenia. Most of the time, he was sweet and docile, but occasionally he would become very violent, threatening the lives of those around him. This client loved her little brother despite his illness. He never became completely well, but eventually medication stopped the violent threats. Later in life, this client married a man who was mentally ill. Her husband was usually sweet (at least for the initial part of their relationship), but eventually he became violent with her, showing the severity of his mental illness. It broke this client's heart to divorce her husband, but she could not continue to endure the abuse. This client exhibited both a trauma bond with her younger brother and unfinished business. Because she felt responsible for not being able to make her brother well, she gave countless chances to her husband in hopes she could make him well and finish the business she was not able to with her younger brother. She also became desensitized to abuse and justified it as due to her husband's mental illness, never holding him accountable for his words and actions.

This principle is also true for relationships outside of marriage. Several years ago, I led a support group for the wives of sex addicts. One woman in the group was very sweet, but she clearly had some kind of judgment regarding rejection. There was just something about her that made me want to reject her. I recognized it and fought hard to counteract this spiritual force. I would watch other people roll their eyes or look away in the group when she was speaking. It was a very strong defilement with her. In terms of the law of attraction, on a subconscious level she expected rejection, rejected herself (because of the continual rejection), and attracted rejection. (Like attracts like.) There was an energetic and spiritual force communicating to everyone in the room to comply with the message of rejection.

This situation created much heartache in me because it was an example of what I see so often: people have a belief system created out of (a) painful event(s) which then perpetually attracts that very thing, reinforcing the "truth" of this belief system. In this woman's case, the belief was, "No one likes me, everyone will reject me." Objectively speaking, she did nothing to deserve this, but I noticed this belief was pervasive in this specific group as most of the women had felt deeply rejected by their husbands.

In many marriages, couples continually defile each other in this manner, attracting what they expect. Often, I hear couples say, "They weren't like this before I married them..." and, truly, this may be the case. These individuals did not exhibit this bitter roots defilement until they "became one" with their spouse through marriage. They may have carried this expectation or energetic belief/judgment into their marriage and the presence of this subconscious, energetic message influenced their spouse to change their perception of and feelings towards the other spouse.

As a holistic practitioner, I look for the bitter root judgement, the unfinished business and the subconscious belief, and address them from different angles. Releasing resentment from the person who may have defiled them, asking God to forgive them for violating the law of judgment, and reprogramming their deeply-rooted subconscious beliefs are steps in changing the repeated manifestation in a person's life. (Repentance means to change your mind, not to say I'm sorry.)

Many Christians have many judgments stored against God as well. These judgments came from disappointments in their relationships with parents (especially fathers) or interpretations of events that included God disappointing them. A common judgment is the belief that because God did not show up in a time of need, He does not care. Again, these beliefs are stored in our subconscious and don't align with truth. The fruit of these beliefs are not aligned with God's promises. Like the numerous scriptures previously quoted (Matthew 9:29, Matthew 21:21, Mark 11:23, Matthew 8:13, John 14:1, James 1:5-8, Philippians 4:6, Matthew 6:25-31), God gives vibrational/spiritual criteria we must follow in order to see our prayers answered, but our soul creates misalignments through experience, causing us to miss the manifestation of His promises.

Most people are not consciously aware they are judging, doing it almost automatically. It is the way of the world. At the very end of the movie "God's Not Dead," we learn that the staunch, God-hating atheist professor had drawn the wrong conclusion about God as a child. His life's mission was to prove God did not exist because of this hurt. If you have seen the movie, you can imagine how differently his life may have looked if he had received healing of this hurt earlier in life and removed the lies, negative beliefs, and judgments he had about God. Many people live less fruitful lives because they are driven by their unresolved hurts, unfinished business, bitter root judgments, and misaligned beliefs.

In general, we are easily offended and can judge quickly. A judgment is usually identifiable because there is a thought such as: "I would never do that." Imagine you are in a grocery store and you see a mom screaming at her child and you think, "What a mean mom, I would never do that." The next day you find yourself yelling at your own child inappropriately. This law (of bitter roots judgements) has just been manifested. This also happens when we make a comparison. In comparing, we either judge the other person or we judge our self. Both conflict with Philippians 4:8 which tells us to only think on good things. It may seem impossible to abstain from judgement, and it certainly is challenging, but the wonderful thing about the way God created us is the ability to repent for our sins, stopping the law in motion and negating it. Repentance means "to change your mind," so when we repent of a judgment, we stop the intentions and change our vibration which changes the attraction.

Mark 11:24-25 says:
"[24]Therefore I tell you, whatever you ask for in prayer, believe that you have received it, and it will be yours. [25]And when you stand praying, if you hold anything against anyone, forgive them, so that your Father in heaven may forgive you your sins."

Holding something against someone is judgment. In Matthew 18:21-35, Jesus tell the parable of the unforgiving servant to explain how often we should forgive those who sin against us:

[21]Then Peter came to Jesus and asked, "Lord, how many times shall I forgive my brother or sister who sins against me? Up to seven times?"
[22]Jesus answered, "I tell you, not seven times, but seventy-seven times."
[23]"Therefore, the kingdom of heaven is like a king who wanted to settle accounts with his servants. [24]As he began the settlement, a man who owed him ten thousand bags of gold was brought to him. [25]Since he was not able to pay, the master ordered that he

and his wife and his children and all that he had be sold to repay the debt."

26 "At this the servant fell on his knees before him. 'Be patient with me,' he begged, 'and I will pay back everything.' 27 The servant's master took pity on him, canceled the debt and let him go.

28 "But when that servant went out, he found one of his fellow servants who owed him a hundred silver coins. He grabbed him and began to choke him. 'Pay back what you owe me!' he demanded."

29 "His fellow servant fell to his knees and begged him, 'Be patient with me, and I will pay it back.'

30 "But he refused. Instead, he went off and had the man thrown into prison until he could pay the debt. 31 When the other servants saw what had happened, they were outraged and went and told their master everything that had happened."

32 "Then the master called the servant in. 'You wicked servant,' he said, 'I canceled all that debt of yours because you begged me to. 33 Shouldn't you have had mercy on your fellow servant just as I had on you?' 34 In anger his master handed him over to the jailers to be tortured, until he should pay back all he owed.

35 "This is how my heavenly Father will treat each of you unless you forgive your brother or sister from your heart."

While there are several interpretations of this parable, Jesus is communicating that we will suffer if we don't forgive because we have been forgiven of so very much by the king (Jesus/God). This is not about eternal salvation, this is about sowing and reaping. If we hold judgment and bitterness in, and don't extend forgiveness and grace, then we will attract judgment in the same manner. If we want grace, we sow grace. If we want to be criticized, we sow criticism. If we want God to answer prayer (which requires grace) then we must release judgment and bitterness and sow grace. Like attracts like. Criticism, judgment, and bitterness vibrate low and don't attract good things. Forgiveness, grace, and faith vibrate high and bring good things.

Do you know the technology behind noise-cancelling headphones? Simply put, the headphones send out a frequency that is exactly opposite of the surrounding frequency, cancelling the surrounding frequency out and creating silence. Repenting and forgiving act on the same principle as noise-cancelling headphones. In effect, they create a cancellation of the frequency. When we judge and are bitter, we send out a low frequency wave. By forgiving and repenting of judgment, we cancel the frequency just sent and set ourselves up in a position to have a higher frequency. One example from my own life was going through a period where I felt rejected by my peers. I walked around vigilant of someone talking about me behind my back or for a glance that communicated rejection. I did some healing work, which included forgiving my peers and repenting for my perception of them as being critical towards me. (This also included healing of my low self-esteem that was a result of rejection.) Somehow, I stopped expecting rejection from other people and it stopped happening. Now, I expect people to like and accept me (in general) and that seems to be the overall experience I have with people. It never crosses my mind that anything is unlikable about me. If people seem to display dislike towards me, I let them have an opinion without undermining my value. I cancelled the negative vibrations from occurring in my life by repenting of my judgement and changing my beliefs and expectations. Do you see repeating patterns in your life? Can you correlate these repeating patterns (bad fruit) to judgments you made at a younger age?

Inner Vows

Another one of Sandford's principles is about "inner vows." We make vows along with judgments. When someone hurts us, we judge them, ourselves, and/or God (or the universe) and, out of fear, we make vows. Making a vow is the exertion of our will over God's which creates a false sense of self-protection. Think about us as sheep under the care of a shepherd. When something bad happens, we think the shepherd is not caring for us, so we leave the safety of the flock and decide to take care of ourselves in this area. This leads to an opening for fear, worry, and control and is the opposite of trust (relying on, adhering to) in God's desire for and direction in the best plan for our life. We begin to doubt His goodness and therefore (we reason), we must control our own life. Because we don't realize other factors have been the cause of bad things happening to us, we determine God or the universe is not for us in this area.

Vows are subconscious determinations of "I will or I will never."

These vows usually have an "I will do whatever it takes to _____." A common example I find is: "I will do whatever it takes to never become an alcoholic like my mother or father." Because this is rooted in fear and judgment, it creates a low vibration in this area and attracts the very thing we don't want to happen, thus reinforcing the untrue belief system the experience created in the first place. It is hard to recognize and acknowledge a lie when our experience has consistently reinforced a certain belief. Consider this example of an inner vow from a woman who had abuse issues in her life. She had vowed she would never let herself be abused again and yet she would consistently attract abusive people (both male and female) into her life. When she cancelled her judgements surrounding trust and protection, spoke truth to her victim mentality, and repented for the vow that she would never be abused again, her life improved greatly. (We did some trapped emotions work and found other vows and judgments as well.) Overall, she started feeling safer around her peers and noticed they began treating her with more respect.

Can you remember thinking in your heart at any point in your life "I will or I will never?"

Blessing

If we take a step past negating bitter root judgments, then we encounter the power of blessing. I highly recommend a current book by Kerry Kirkwood called *The Power of Blessing*.[xxii] If repenting of judgment and forgiving have the effect of releasing us from the consequences of judgment (per the law of bitter root judgments), then when we take our process one step further by blessing that person, we can create a powerful vibration by sowing something positive in place of a negative. The word "blessing" in Hebrew translates to "barak," and in Greek translates to "eulogia." It means "to speak God's intention." When we bless, we vibrate on God's frequency. If our intention can change water molecules, then imagine what God's intention does! James 3:5; 9-10 says:

> [5]Likewise, the tongue is a small part of the body, but it makes great boasts. Consider what a great forest is set on fire by a small spark... [9] With the tongue we praise our Lord and Father, and with it we curse human beings, who have been made in God's likeness. [10]Out of the same mouth come praise and cursing. My brothers and sisters, this should not be.

God's intention is to bless. We are made in His image. When we curse, we are not operating in our true identity and we create a negative vibration which attracts negative things to us. We undermine our given authority and are making judgments. As stated earlier, when we judge, we reap bad fruit back upon us, whether it is in word, thought, and/or intention. When we repent and make the conscious effort to bless, we negate the reaping of bad fruit. When we bless, we sow God's intention and we reap a great reward for blessing.

Many throw around the term "repentance" and believe it to be a synonym for the act of saying "I'm sorry" and/or to turn away from sinful behavior. The actual definition of repentance is "to change your mind" or change your belief. It isn't just saying sorry, it is changing what you think and intend. Blessing requires more than just our casual definition of repentance (to say sorry); it requires we move into a whole different space of love, joy, gratitude, and peace. In order to bless, we actually have to think/intend something good towards the other person, not just act humbly about our own mistakes. This is a new step that has a great effect in terms of attraction.

You may say something like, "How do I bless the guy who has raped my daughter?" or "I am supposed to bless my father who abandoned me, my mother, and my siblings for another woman?" I get it, in these circumstance (and many others), it is not easy to do. Blessing in this circumstance could take the form of a prayer or declaration. For example, you could declare: "I bless the life of the man who defiled my daughter so that God could use his crime to bring some kind of healing and transformation (to him or someone else). I bless that God could turn his story into a miraculous testimony." This is much like declaring Romans 8:28. Isn't this much more empowering? Having said that, we must recognize that some offenses are easier to let go of than others. The end result should be that our response creates a positive ripple effect. God said to Abraham in Genesis 12:3 (AMP):

> "And I will bless those who bless you [who confer prosperity or happiness upon you] and curse him who curses or uses insolent language toward you; in you will all the families and kindred of the earth be blessed [and by you they will bless themselves]."

In this verse, God was specifically talking about the Jews. But are we not all God's children because of the price Jesus paid? Are we not all "grafted into the vine" as believers? I believe this principle truly transfers to all men. Theologians will say that Jesus took on all our curses so that curses are not part of the New Covenant. What if we substituted the concept of sowing and reaping in place of cursing? If you judge or curse someone, you will reap bad fruit.

You may say, "But what if someone is truly evil?" Well, the Bible calls Satan, "the accuser of the Brethren" (Revelations 12:10) and we are to see evil as operating through someone because of demonic forces and not actually view the person as evil themselves. Ephesians 6:12 (New King James Version) says:

> For we do not wrestle against flesh and blood, but against principalities, against powers, against the rulers of the darkness of

this age, against spiritual hosts of wickedness in the heavenly places.

It would be easier to separate the person from the evil spiritual force operating through them or deceiving them if we make a point to remember the war is not within this physical realm. We all have flesh and the capacity for evil and we all require God's grace and mercy. "There but for the grace of God, go I" (one of my favorite quotes by John Bradford, a famous leader of the Pilgrims). Satan's greatest delight is to separate brothers in Christ. He knows the power of unity. If he can keep us upset with one another, we lose the power of the kingdom (remember, peace and joy). Staying offended guarantees that we keep our vibration low, reap bad fruit, miss blessings, and that God doesn't forgive our sins (Matthew 6:15). Forgiving, repenting, and blessing in every situation that comes our way ensures we stay in a state of peace and joy, are in God's will, vibrate high, create expansion by giving energy to and, ultimately, reap positive things. Are you practicing any of these steps? Are you complaining and problem focused? Look around at our world's current state and ask, "How's that working for us?" I hate to say it, but I don't think what we have been doing has been working well (in general). Maybe it's time to try a different strategy to change the world. My hope is that if enough people truly get the principles stated in this book, and begin to implement them, we can change things.

Matthew 7 also ties these ideas together. The first verses in this chapter are about judgement and taking the "log" out of our own eye (Matthew 7:4-5 NIV). Immediately following this, Jesus says:

> "[7]Ask and it will be given to you; seek and you will find; knock and the door will be opened to you. [8]For everyone who asks receives; the one who seeks finds; and to the one who knocks, the door will be opened. [9]Which of you, if your son asks for bread, will give him a stone? [10]Or if he asks for a fish, will give him a snake? [11]If you, then, though you are evil, know how to give good gifts to your children, how much more will your Father in heaven

give good gifts to those who ask him! [12]So in everything, do to others what you would have them do to you, for this sums up the Law and the Prophets."

Once again, we see this alignment about getting what we ask God for when we stay clean of bitter root judgments and when we bless others (verse 12). I believe there is a direct correlation between judging/being critical of others and not seeing our prayers answered. When we live a life free of offense, we vibrate higher. The verse in between those discussing judgement and petition introduces another interesting concept. Matthew 7:6 says:

"Do not give dogs what is sacred; do not throw your pearls to pigs. If you do, they may trample them under their feet, and turn and tear you to pieces."

Not throwing pearls to swine has generally been understood as not sharing things which are holy with people who don't understand them. In between the contexts of Matthew 7:1 and Matthew 7:7 ("Ask and it will be given to you; seek and you will find; knock and the door will be opened to you."), I would suggest this verse means to avoid people who don't understand the principle of bitter root judgements; those who are highly judgmental, critical, and gossip about others. (We might identify this as a "religious spirit.") Hanging out with people with a "religious spirit" may cause us to fall into a judgemental state and, thus, not receiving the fruit of Matthew 7:7. Hanging out with gossipers is rarely a high vibration environment. If your peers don't make a conscious effort to avoid practicing the law of bitter root judgments, don't hang out with them. They just might suck you in...

CHAPTER 6
SCRIPTURES SUPPORTING THE
LAW OF EXPANSION

The law of expansion in quantum physics says that whatever you focus on, you give power to and it gets bigger or expands. So if I add mental and emotional energy to a problem, the problem will expand. When I add mental/emotional energy to a solution, the solution gets bigger and expands. You can imagine this in many visuals, for example, throwing flames into an existing fire or adding water into a tub that is already overflowing.

When we consider all the scriptures already mentioned pertaining to sowing and reaping and what we focus our intentions on, it makes sense that God would be so intentional in the New Testament to educate us on the power of our thoughts, words, and prayers.

When we combine the law of reciprocity with the law of expansion, we can see that what we give energy to, we empower, and it grows. Remember, we get back what we give, multiplied. A small amount of yeast allows a lot of dough to expand. It is interesting that Jesus also talks about bad yeast (the Pharisees) in Matthew 16:5-12, proving the law of expansion works in the negative too. Sowing positive energy causes our positive attractions to expand and sowing negative energy causes our negative attractions to expand. Remember what Job said in Job 3:25:

> What I feared has come upon me; what I dreaded has happened to me.

Scripture indicates that much of Job's devotion was out of fear of something bad happening to him or God's punishment. This fear was the open door that gave Satan legal ground to afflict Job (Job 3:25).

Remember, Jesus repeatedly tells us not to fear in the gospels. When we focus on fear, shame, guilt, or other low frequency energies or emotions, we expand those things which are already negative and/or attract new sources of negativity. In this way, we manifest our circumstances based on what or where we give energy. When we focus on joy, gratitude, purpose, health, abundance, and peace, we energize and attract both existing and new positive things into our lives. When we add the law of expansion to the law of reciprocity, we derive the Biblical law of sowing and reaping, where things are not only returned (reciprocity), but have been multiplied. This should be your motivation to begin paying attention to your thoughts, emotions, beliefs, words, and so on.

The Law of Attraction vs. Prayer

Have you ever thought about the difference between prayer and intention? It is common to think that God only hears our prayers and that unless we address Him first, He will ignore the thoughts we have in our minds. Remember, if the water experiments had the same effect with intentions as words, then our thoughts about ourselves and others carry the same power as our words. This bears repeating. If you curse someone in your thoughts, you have cursed them in your words. If you bless someone in your thoughts, you bless them with your words. **Intention carries the same weight as words.** James 3:10 says we should not bless and curse with the same tongue. Do we do this in our thoughts?

One of the techniques you can use to successfully apply the law of attraction to your life could be:

1. You decide what you want (general or specific).
2. You think, feel, imagine, and see that thing coming to pass. You must have a burning desire for this thing to manifest. Your feelings are very important. Be very detailed. The brain cannot discern between real experiences and visualization (the same neurons fire under both conditions). You are creating a specific

vibration for what you want to manifest. You want to focus on how having this will make you feel.

3. You repeat this exercise with the same intensity. You don't worry about the how it will come to pass and you don't demand a time frame.

4. When your belief lines up with your feelings (you know it will happen) then it will happen.[xxiii]

This technique differs from that of *The Secret* which states to ask only once and believe. In my opinion, the law of attraction requires you to continue putting forth the effort/work until you really believe it will happen. Again, this lines up with scripture like Matthew 7:7 and Philippians 4:6.

> Philippians 4:6 (AMP) says:
> Do not fret or have any anxiety about anything, but in every circumstance and in everything, by prayer and petition ([a] definite requests), with thanksgiving, continue to make your wants known to God.

At first glance, this verse may seem like a direct contradiction to *The Secret,* which says we should only ask once for the things we want, but it is not. By continually making our wants known to God, we are not asking just for the sake of asking, we are activating our faith until we are able to let go of the anxiety that it will be answered.

We are constantly sowing every moment of every day, even in our silence. We spend time in deliberate prayer asking God to answer our requests, but then we negate our prayers, like noise-cancelling headphones, by thinking negatively. If thoughts do indeed become things, then we pray negatively every time we dwell on negative things. Let's say my daughter strikes me as being extremely strong-willed and stubborn, and it occurs to me she is making bad choices in her life. If I am praying fervently that she will listen to good advice and make better choices, but my thoughts and words are declaring that she is being stubborn and making bad choices, then I am negating my own prayers with opposite frequencies. I am undoing the positive of my prayers because I am not really praying in faith.

Do not be confused...this process does not invalidate my need to manage the negative emotions that come along with certain circumstances. I may need to ask, "What meaning did I give to this behavior? Did it make me feel worthless, rejected, betrayed, devalued, or like a failure? Have these feelings occurred before under different circumstances?" Once I have successfully found the roots to these issues and processed all the negative emotions, it is required that I move in faith, avoid neutralizing my prayers and beliefs with complaining or criticizing, and, ultimately, forgive my daughter for how her choices have hurt or offended me. Has it occurred to you to use this process when you are offended? This is the beginning step to mindfulness.

If we truly embrace the idea that every intention/thought we have is the same as a prayer, perhaps we would be more conscious of our thoughts. Remember Paul said to "pray without ceasing" in 1 Thessalonians 5:17. Perhaps Paul was making us aware that if God sees no distinction between thoughts and prayers, then our thoughts need to be as deliberate as our prayers.

Before I knew about the law of attraction, I would joke that when I prayed or asked God for something, I had to stop myself from imagining how He would bring it to pass because He would always do it in a way I had not imagined. I decided I would save Him the energy of having to create an unusual way to answer my prayer by not trying to figure out how He was going to answer it. In the law of attraction methodology, trying to figure out the "how" takes out the trust, faith, and belief in the process and imposes doubt. Attempting to control the "how" affects the manifestation and reflects doubt, worry, and fear. Remember what it says in The Lord's Prayer in Matthew 6:9-13 (NIV):

" [9]This, then, is how you should pray:
'Our Father in heaven,
hallowed be your name,

61

¹⁰**Your kingdom** come,

Your **will** be done,

on earth as it is in heaven.' "

Earlier I defined the kingdom of God in Romans 14:17 (peace and joy) and the will of God in Ephesians 5:17 (peace, hymns, encouragement).^{xxiv} Heaven is a place of peace and joy and our prayers make Heaven come to earth. Jesus said in Luke 17:21 that the kingdom of God is within us. In essence, when we pray, we are saying that we want to vibrate high like Heaven vibrates. I believe when our vibration is high (like in Heaven) then we see the things we pray for manifest on earth.

1 Peter 3:7 (AMP) says:

In the same way you married men should live considerately with [your wives], with an intelligent recognition [of the marriage relation], honoring the woman as [physically] the weaker, but [realizing that you] are joint heirs of the grace (God's unmerited favor) of life, in order that your prayers may not be hindered and cut off. [Otherwise you cannot pray effectively].

The word "hindered" here means to cut down a fruit-bearing tree.^{xxv} This reminds me of the noise-cancelling headphones. Because you are one with your spouse, when you do not honor him/her (with good intentions), you cut off the effectiveness of your prayers for him/her. (They bear no fruit.) We cannot allow unresolved offenses to cause us to think badly about our spouse and then expect our prayer for them to be effective. The good and bad intentions cancel one another out. I believe the same is true of our children and anyone we may have authority over. Recent books and teachings on the "Courts of Heaven" have laid out these exact same principles. When we "open doors" to negative things, our words, beliefs, and prayers do not align.^{xxvi}

Remember the faith chapters I discussed earlier? They seem to imply that we can manifest things by faith (i.e. move mountains). We see this dance of the concepts of faith, asking, belief, prayer, intention, words, and so on. They are all interconnected. Remember the supposition that God lets the universe run (to a great degree) by the law of attraction? So we can think of prayer is an exercise of the law of attraction, and if we follow God's criteria, we will see prayers answered.

How does this change your perspective on prayer?

Blessing and Scales of Justice

Old Testament law required a thief who has been caught to repay his debt two, five, or seven times (Exodus 22:1; 22:4; Leviticus 6:5, 22:14, Proverbs 6:31b). When Satan or another person steals from us, God promises to bring justice, but this is hinged on us fully trusting Him to bring it to pass and not taking matters into our own hands. This involves not judging (or repenting for judgements made) and blessing. When we judge or curse, and especially slander, we become the thief. God brings justice to our accused by blessing them and we get bad fruit. We see this illustrated in 2 Samuel 16:5-14 (NIV):

As King David approached Bahurim, a man from the same clan as Saul's family came out from there. His name was Shimei son of Gera, and he cursed as he came out. [6]He pelted David and all the king's officials with stones, though all the troops and the special guard were on David's right and left. [7]As he cursed, Shimei said, "Get out, get out, you murderer, you scoundrel! [8]The LORD has repaid you for all the blood you shed in the household of Saul, in whose place you have reigned. The LORD has given the kingdom into the hands of your son Absalom. You have come to ruin because you are a murderer!" [9]Then Abishai son of Zeruiah said to the king, "Why should this dead dog curse my lord the king? Let me go over and cut off his head." [10]But the king said, "What does this have to do with you, you sons of Zeruiah? If he is cursing because the LORD said to him, 'Curse David,' who can ask, 'why do you do this?' " [11]David then said to Abishai and all his officials, "My son, my own flesh and blood, is trying to kill me.

How much more, then, this Benjamite! Leave him alone; let him curse, for the LORD has told him to. [12]It may be that the LORD will look upon my misery and restore to me his covenant blessing instead of his curse today."

David knew the principle of justice. If they didn't retaliate, then David was set up for God to bring justice and blessing.

Romans 12:19 says:
Do not take revenge, my dear friends, but leave room for God's wrath, for it is written: "It is mine to avenge; I will repay," says the Lord.

When we forgive, repent for judging, bless, and don't take revenge, we set ourselves up for God to bless us and take vengeance upon our enemies. But remember that they too are God's children (and we war not against flesh and blood). Just because it occurs to us that what someone does is evil, doesn't make it so. God desires for them to come to repentance also. They will reap what they sow according to Galatians 6:7, so we don't have to take revenge. By staying in a state of bitterness, resentment, and judgment, we ensure that we will be "turned over to the tormentors." We lower our vibration and thus should expect to reap what we sowed in our reaction to them.

Jesus said in Luke 6:27-28 (AMP):
"But I say to you who are listening now to Me: [in order to heed, make it a practice to] love your enemies, treat well (do good to, act nobly toward) those who detest you and pursue you with hatred, [28]invoke blessings upon and pray for the happiness of those who curse you, implore God's blessing (favor) upon those who abuse you [who revile, reproach, disparage, and high-handedly misuse you]."

Wow, imagine how hard this is to do! Here, Jesus is conferring a spiritual principle to us. If someone curses, persecutes, or slanders us (remember the beatitudes in Matthew 5:11), and we do not retaliate with bitterness, hatred, judgment, or cursing, then God blesses us as part of the law of justice. God operates within His justice system (most of the time). When we go into the courtroom of Heaven, "the accuser of the brethren" or Satan (Revelations 12:10) brings our laundry list of offenses, but we bring the new covenant with Jesus as our defense. Our sins are forgiven if we repent and forgive our offender (according to Mark 11:4). This dismantles the argument of the prosecutor and rules in our favor, awarding us recompense for what was taken from us. So, if we suffer, choose to forgive, release the "thief," and ask God for recompense, He will grant it to us. He is waiting for us to ask Him (through our words, intentions, heart's desires, or beliefs) to restore what was taken. Justice is a high law that seems to trump many others, but still there is a law higher than the law of justice.

I have seen many people's lives changed because they forgive, repent (changed their minds), and bless. I have had many clients (male and female; this is not a gender issue) who have repeatedly attracted the same types of relationships with the same negative outcomes. Through therapy sessions, I taught them very detailed and specific ways to forgive the hurts caused by their dysfunctional partners. These clients realized they held deep judgment and bitterness in their hearts towards their past partners that created strong beliefs about men/women in general. After changing those deep-rooted beliefs and judgements and practicing blessing, many of these clients would contact me with the news that they were dating someone wonderful who was very unlike the past partners they had attracted. When they realized they were not just victims, but that they had held beliefs that allowed abusive and toxic people to come into their lives, they took responsibility to change. They believed they could actually get what they wanted and were not just going to live life feeling victimized.

This process works. I have had many clients whose lives are completely different from using this process. If you knew every decision you made was going to work out for you in a positive way, what would you do differently? How would you feel if you rested in knowing you can't "screw it up"?

Gratitude

Gratitude is focusing on positive energy with thoughts and words. Gratitude is thinking about the things for which we are thankful instead of the things not going well for us. Many people are able to practice gratitude by pivoting. Pivoting is recognizing you are stuck in negative thinking and deliberately changing your intention to something positive for which you are thankful for. Many people report immediately feeling a shift in their emotions when doing this. What causes that?

Isaiah 61:3 (NIV) says:
...and provide for those who grieve in Zion-- to bestow on them a crown of beauty instead of ashes, the oil of joy instead of mourning, and a garment of praise instead of a spirit of despair.

Philippians 4:6 says:
Do not be anxious about anything, but in every situation, by prayer and petition, with thanksgiving, present your requests to God.

1 Thessalonians 5:16-18 says:
[16]Rejoice always, [17]pray continually, [18]give thanks in all circumstances; for this is God's will for you in Christ Jesus.

Energetically, when we are thinking negative thoughts, we are literally making ourselves weak by internally directing negative energy waves towards ourselves. I demonstrate this with every new client using muscle testing. I will instruct them to say and think something negative about themselves, and when they do, their muscles test weak. I will then instruct them to say and think something positive about themselves, and when they do, their muscles test strong. This is the perfect demonstation of the power our thoughts have over our whole being. We think an average of 60,000 thoughts a day. Think about how many of them might be negative. Every negative thought creates weakness.

Other research from authors such as Caroline Leaf show that negative thoughts actually produce "toxic trees" in the brain.[xxvii] Energy medicine agrees that our thoughts produce disease. A recent Netflix movie called "Heal" documents these concepts in real cases.

There is an interesting story that shows up in three out of four of the gospels. The version in Luke 7:38-50 reads:

[36]When one of the Pharisees invited Jesus to have dinner with him, he went to the Pharisee's house and reclined at the table. [37]A woman in that town who lived a sinful life learned that Jesus was eating at the Pharisee's house, so she came there with an alabaster jar of perfume. [38]As she stood behind him at his feet weeping, she began to wet his feet with her tears. Then she wiped them with her hair, kissed them and poured perfume on them.

[39]When the Pharisee who had invited him saw this, he said to himself, "If this man were a prophet, he would know who is touching him and what kind of woman she is—that she is a sinner."

[40]Jesus answered him, "Simon, I have something to tell you."

'"Tell me, teacher," he said.

[41]"Two people owed money to a certain moneylender. One owed him five hundred denarii and the other fifty. [42]Neither of them had the money to pay him back, so he forgave the debts of both. Now which of them will love him more?"

[43]Simon replied, "I suppose the one who had the bigger debt forgiven."

"You have judged correctly," Jesus said.

[44]Then he turned toward the woman and said to Simon, "Do you see this woman? I came into your house. You did not give me any water for my feet, but she wet my feet with her tears and wiped them with her hair. [45]You did not give me a kiss, but this woman, from the time I entered, has not stopped kissing my feet. [46]You did not put oil on my head, but she has poured perfume on my

feet. ⁴⁷Therefore, I tell you, her many sins have been forgiven—as her great love has shown. But whoever has been forgiven little loves little."

⁴⁸Then Jesus said to her, "Your sins are forgiven."

⁴⁹The other guests began to say among themselves, "Who is this who even forgives sins?"

⁵⁰Jesus said to the woman, "Your faith has saved you; go in peace."

The same story is told in Matthew 26:12-13 in which Jesus says:

¹² "When she poured this perfume on my body, she did it to prepare me for burial. ¹³Truly I tell you, wherever this gospel is preached throughout the world, what she has done will also be told, in memory of her."

Simon's role in this story highlights the principle of entitlement and is an example of how we should not act. He was haughty and proud and did not understand the gravity of this woman's reckless pouring out of the most valuable thing she had to show her gratitude to Jesus. He was stuck in the bitter root judgment of her sinfulness, which reflected on his own pride. Jesus did not commend Simon for his faith, but contrasted his lack of manners towards his guests, his pride, and his judgment to the woman's act of faith. Her frequency was much higher than that of the "sinless" Pharisee.

Is there a story about you in the Bible? Although this woman's name is omitted, her story made it into the gospels. Some believe the bottle of spikenard, an expensive oil used for burial, that she poured on Jesus' feet cost her a years' wages. Have you ever spent that much showing your gratitude to Jesus or anyone else? Imagine how high her frequency was in that moment. Imagine what power was coming from her heart in this humble act of pure devotion.

This woman's story is mentioned in three out of the four gospels in the Bible. She was a nobody whose actions of gratitude and vibrations at the highest possible frequency made her a role model. Songs have even been written about her. It was truly a "sacrifice of praise" for her, costing her an unimaginable price. Gratitude is often costly and it doesn't always feel appropriate. When we are hurting or have just experienced a huge loss or devastation, we are comforted by our sadness and self-pity. In many ways, it feels like a sacrifice to focus on things for which we are grateful, but from a quantum physics standpoint, we energetically make a huge leap in vibration when we do this. If we can program ourselves to do this on a moment-to-moment basis, we can truly reset our brain chemistry and bring ourselves to consistent contentment, regardless of the circumstances. From a law of attraction standpoint, we will begin to attract better things when we focus on higher frequency thoughts and feelings.

CHAPTER 7
SCRIPTURES SUPPORTING THE
LAW OF ENTRAINMENT

Have you ever witnessed an opera singer break a glass with her voice and wondered how that actually happens? This is an example of the principle of resonance and entrainment. When you hit a glass with a fork or knife, it makes a sound. This sound is actually the noise the glass would make if you could hear its vibration. The opera singer hits the note at the same frequency as the glass creating resonance. The glass cannot contain double the resonance of its vibration, so it shatters. This is the principle of entrainment at work. "In essence, entrainment refers to a natural phenomenon in which one entity resonates synchronously with another in response to its dominant frequency of vibration. And whether this resonance occurs on a gross or subtle level, it invariably involves *rhythm*."[xxviii]

Dan McCollum, a seasoned worship leader, pastor, and author, discusses the principles of sound frequency in music and scripture in his book *God Vibrations Study Guide: A Kingdom Perspective on the Power of Sound.*[xxix] McCollum reveals that seismologists have discovered that by taking the frequencies of the earth and attaching them to a musical scale, the earth actually sings like it says in Psalm 66:4. Did you know that the same is true for your DNA? If you tune your DNA to a musical scale, you will produce a song that sings the vibrations of your unique DNA code.

Have you ever heard something and said, "That resonates as true." Again, the feeling you get when something you hear aligns with the frequency your soul senses is the same. Entrainment is how a few people, like an acapella group, singing can sound like many more. Entrainment is when people (or things) resonate at the same vibration.

In the metronome experiment, researchers set 100 metronomes at different speeds on a floating platform. Within a couple of minutes, all the metronomes were going at the same pace. While this is related to principles of oscillation, not entrainment, the wave patterns of the metronomes eventually synchronized with each other. Experiments using pendulums in clocks and other similar devices have shown to have almost identical results, reinforcing this principle.[xxx]

Another example of this principle happens when women move in together as roommates. The close contact eventually causes their menstrual cycles to become entrained (meaning their PMS is also entrained...yikes). This instance alone supports the theory that we are automatically synchronized to those around us. There is an invisible realm of energy around us, affecting us both positively and negatively, and we are naturally driven to resonate with the energy waves it carries.

If you pluck the string of a guitar in your hands while there is another guitar sitting nearby, the same note will start to vibrate in both guitars. If you stop the vibrations of the guitar in your hands, leaving the idle guitar alone, the vibrations from the guitar sitting nearby will eventually synchronize with the strings of the guitar in your hands. Waves are driven to entrain.

If I sent ten people into a room together to measure their individual and total energy, I would see the frequency waves of each person colliding. This is constructive interference. The differing energetic waves bounce back and forth looking to align. Eventually, the predominant frequency in the room will affect the others and all existing waves will synchronize to the dominant frequency. If you went into a room where the majority of the people were complaining, you would eventually begin to feel ungrateful. If you find yourself around sad and depressed people all the time, you may develop a personal struggle with the same thing. Like the metronome experiment, the waves desire to synchronize/entrain in resonance.[xxxi] Benjamin Franklin said, "He who lies with dogs will get up with fleas." This is a perfect example of the principle of entrainment as it applies to the company one keeps. (Ironically, Franklin was a hedonist, so he would know about this firsthand.)

1 Corinthians 15:33 (NASB) says:
Do not be deceived: "Bad company corrupts good morals."

Proverbs 14:7 says:
Leave the presence of a fool, Or you will not discern words of knowledge.

Psalm 26:4-5 says:
I do not sit with deceitful men, Nor will I go with pretenders. I hate the assembly of evildoers, And I will not sit with the wicked.

Psalm 1:1-3 reads:
[1]How blessed is the man who does not walk in the counsel of the wicked, Nor stand in the path of sinners, Nor sit in the seat of scoffers! [2]But his delight is in the law of the LORD, And in His law he meditates day and night. [3]He will be like a tree firmly planted by streams of water, Which yields its fruit in its season And its leaf does not wither; And in whatever he does, he prospers.

Proverbs 22:24-25 says:
[24]Do not associate with a man given to anger; Or go with a hot-tempered man, [25]Or you will learn his ways And find a snare for yourself.

While we might talk about these scriptures in terms of demonic influence, it can also be understood in terms of vibration. When we are around negative and depressed people all the time, we may find ourselves being brought down. Being around anxious people may result in feeling anxious. If there is a place for our vibration to entrain with theirs, it may do that. We should limit our interaction to those whom we can either influence or are on a level equal to us. I deal with a number of clients who are energetically sensitive. In other words, they cannot be around many types of people (or electronics) because other people's negative energy overwhelms them. As we raise our vibration, we are less affected by others' lower vibrations and emotions. The same is true with demonic spirits. As we raise our vibration, demonic/low vibration spirits cannot find a place to "entrain." We could compare this principle to the concept of "legal ground" and open doors. Many books and inner healing modalities (such as the Freedom and Fullness process from Vision Life Ministries) use the principles of "legal ground" or open doors.[xxxii] As we "close doors," we spiritually, mentally, emotionally, and physically close the areas of our life that allow these spirits to afflict us. I spend a good bit of time "closing doors" with clients. From a quantum physics perspective, we are "raising the vibration" of the client by releasing the lower vibrational blockages in their life and adding lifestyle changes to raise their overall vibration.

Energy and Frequency Technology

Energy and frequency technology that uses the principles of entrainment has been used for many decades to address symptoms of disease. Royal Rife, the inventor of the Rife machine, proved he could use technology to generate a frequency that when entrained with a kidney stone, would shatter it. This led to the discovery that the frequency of certain medications can be measured and reproduced as a form of treatment without the side effects of chemicals. Rife effectively treated cancer and other pathogens by matching frequencies.

In Lynn McTaggart's *The Intention Experiment* (which will be discussed in detail later), McTaggart presents research where the drug Heparin (which is used for blood coagulation) and the same frequency waves it produces were used in two separate cases to test whether the frequency waves had the same effect as the drug itself. The study found that the frequency produced the same effect in statistically significant outcomes without the typical side effects encountered by using the drug itself.[xxxiii] Today, there are many devices which use vibration and sound technology to impact the body with frequency to either restore a frequency that is out of alignment or to disrupt the frequency of a pathogen in the body. This is the future of energy medicine.

The Zyto[xxxiv] and Asyra[xxxv] scanning devices use frequencies from your hands to measure any deficits you may have in your body and any frequencies that seem to be off. Based on these frequencies, the devices offer recommendations of specific supplements to resolve any issues. An incredible new technology called the "Healy" is a personal machine that runs through a program on your cell phone to record various frequencies in your body throughout the day. After measuring and registering your body's frequencies, the Healy creates counter frequencies to bring your body back into harmony (if necessary). In other words, the software knows which frequencies are harmonious in your body and which ones are not. When it reads a disharmonious frequency, it counters that frequency to correct it. This device is actually permitted to make health claims in Europe, something the Food and Drug Administration rarely allows in the U.S. with products in the alternative health field.[xxxvi]

The Healy, Zyto, Asyra, and any other energy technologies are not magic pills. Although they have the ability to harmonize with your body, they cannot find the original cause of disharmony. These technologies do not substitute for conscious involvement in changed thinking and lifestyle habits and the processing of negative emotions. They are, however, an amazing compliment to consciously changing lifestyle habits and are proven to help your body restore balance (using the law of entrainment), freeing your mind to make other necessary changes quickly, easily, and effectively.

Sound Therapy, Vibrational Technology, and Color Frequencies

Like we saw in Dr. Emoto's experiments, music/sound make a big impact on the water molecules. Sound vibration immediately impacts 60-70% of the body. Harmony is the homeostasis of the body and cells. The brain functions at its peak when synchronized. Disharmony leads to disease. Currently, the American Medical Association agrees that most disease is related to stress, which is caused by disharmony. Sound, music, and the human voice entrains with the natural frequencies of the body, restoring harmony/ease and synchronicity. Sound therapy is designed to restore harmony/entrainment where the cells are out of harmony/entrainment.

Sound therapy studies using both human voices and instruments have revealed some highly therapeutic benefits. The human voice can help reduce the agitation of the autonomic nervous system, which is linked to many inflammatory diseases. There are many diseases today that cannot be linked to a pathogenic origin and therefore cannot be relieved by traditional medicine. There are many diseases today that cannot be linked to a pathogenic origin and therefore cannot be relieved by traditional medicine.

Frequencies can be infused in water and used to heal injuries. Sound therapy is the same as vibrational therapy. All of these principles are built on the same concept. Vibrations and frequencies remediate, align, or disrupt. Light and sound are both different forms of waves. Our eyes pick up light frequencies and our ears hear a limited range of sound frequencies. "Laboratory tests have shown that specific frequencies within the range of the human voice and their harmonics can re-form destabilized water molecules back to structural integrity and that this, in turn, can significantly improve the performance of in vitro DNA."[xxxvii]

Sound therapy devices, like the Huso Machine, send a tone created from human voices, to harmonize the body in certain areas. The out of harmony frequencies synchronize or entrain with the Huso's frequencies. This device is used through both the ears and pulse spots on the wrist or ankle to send harmonizing frequencies into the body that especially help the vagus nerve to be in a neutral and harmonized state. [xxxviii] Other options in vibrational therapy include Wholetones, a sound therapy based on the frequency of specific music notes.[xxxix] The purpose is to entrain and harmonize the body's natural frequencies that may have been disrupted by various factors.[xl]

The Evox (made by Zyto) is a frequency machine with a proprietary program that scans the content of the voice for any frequency deficits. The device works by the participant speaking into a microphone and the computer revealing any unresolved issues, trauma energy, trapped

75

emotions or beliefs, and potential deficits in various organs of the body based on voice frequencies.[xli] The power of this concept is key. Your voice contains your life story and is a unique signature of your health and, therefore, an indicator of any unresolved traumas/issues. This signature changes as you transform positively or negatively. Our authority is contained in the release of our voice and our thoughts. If we can successfully manage a major emotional, physical, mental, and spiritual life change, our voice can actually change, positively or negatively.

Remember: we are body, soul, and spirit. Everything we have ever thought, said, experienced, and acted upon is registered within our subconscious and measured in the vibration of our body and voice. Jesus says in Mark 11:23:

> "Truly I tell you, if anyone says to this mountain, 'Go throw yourself into the sea' and does not doubt in their heart but believe that what they say will happen, it will be done for them."

So, when we make holistic wellness (the wellness and harmony of our body, soul, and spirit) a priority, we actually change the power of our voice.

Color frequencies are another way we entrain. We have discussed light having various frequencies that manifest to the human eye in different colors. In color therapy, the vibrations of specific colors are used to remediate symptoms that respond well to those particular colors. The seven colors of the rainbow also align with the seven chakra or emotion centers of the body. Each vibration gets progressively higher from the root to the crown center of the chakra. When combined, they create white light. Often, a person will be missing a color and need that vibration. Intuitively, we are drawn to colors we need if we are listening to our gut. Our body will tell us the colors we need to balance our energy centers in our body.

Quantum energy medicine has harnessed the concepts of sound, light, and vibration to create therapeutic devices designed to entrain with the body's created harmonies. When the body is in disharmony or is experiencing disease, these devices will encourage the body, using entrainment, to return to their designed harmonious frequencies.

Entrainment with Others

The most powerful principle of entrainment can be seen in the Word. It says in Deuteronomy 32:30 that, "one will put one thousand to flight," (meaning demons), "but two will put ten thousand to flight." This scripture is teaching us that when men are in unity, the effects of their prayers are exponentially magnified. From sound theory, resonance would promote entrainment and entrainment magnifies the outcome or effect, but how easy is it to entrain with someone else? We see an example of this in the story of Jericho in Joshua 6. As the Israelites silently march in perfect unison and then, all of the sudden, shout contemporaneously, we see the principles of sound theory and entrainment at work. Could the power of their unified obedience have resulted in a physical collapse of the walls?

We can scientifically say "yes". The bridge at Broughton, near Manchester, England, was built in 1826 in the new "suspension" style. Being one of Europe's first suspension bridges, and only five-years-old, it was considered state-of-the-art. Soon after its construction, British troops marched "in time" in 4 columns across the bridge. Their synchronized footsteps began a rhythmic resonance creating a pleasant sort of bounce, causing some of the men to start whistling in time! Unfortunately, the troops did not realize that the bouncing resonance created more and more up and down movement of the bridge until the structure started crumbling and collapsed, taking the soldiers with it.

Why do you think King David ordered a massive group of musicians and singers to engage in 24/7 praise and worship in the temple? Could it be he had a revelation that the frequency of the minstrels aligned with the vibration of Heaven? Perhaps he understood a portal to Heaven was opened when there was entrainment and resonance from men vibrating at a specific unified frequency. Why do we start church services with praise and worship? It raises the frequency in unity and opens up the Heavens for us to experience God's presence.

If a group of believers gathers with unresolved offenses amongst one another, they send interference waves and block entrainment. Can you see then the incredible importance of Matthew 18 and other scriptures that teach about walking in peace with our brothers and sisters in Christ? Jesus repeatedly reminds us of the importance of clearing offenses among each other because we are all connected through Him. If you read the gospels, focusing on this concept, you'll find it shows up frequently in His teachings.

Now, imagine if a group of entrained believers, who have learned how to raise their vibration to the kingdom of God (peace and joy according to Romans 14:17) gather and seek the Lord's heart. They have resolved any conflict amongst each other, carry no offense or unforgiveness towards one another, and genuinely believe their prayers will make an impact. Imagine if they set their corporate intention, while entrained, to bring transformational solutions. What would that look like? What do you imagine the outcome to be? Matthew 18:19 says:

> "Again I say to you, that if two of you agree on earth about anything that they may ask, it shall be done for them by My Father who is in heaven."

Why isn't prayer answered? Because we are not aligning with the criteria set forth in scripture and discussed here. We are not entrained with one another in unity. The practices laid out in this book are designed to raise our vibration in assurance that we are in true unity and that God will do "anything" we agree upon, as long as it aligns with His truths.

CHAPTER 8
THE HIERARCHIES IN THE LAWS

O n earth, we see many different laws in operation. The law of gravity keeps us from floating away while preventing us from flying. The law of aerodynamics trumps the law of gravity allowing birds, planes, and Superman to fly. This suggests that laws function according to a hierarchy, with some laws overriding others. I am sure physicists have many examples of this. This is true in the kingdom of God as well. James 2:13 (NIV) reads:

> ...because judgment without mercy will be shown to anyone who has not been merciful. Mercy triumphs over judgment.

As discussed, when we judge (don't show mercy) then we reap judgment (without mercy). Because of the scales of justice being in balance, we create a space to receive mercy and blessing when someone else judges or curses us. So mercy, which vibrates high, trumps judgment. I call this the law of grace and mercy.

Grace is receiving good things we *don't* deserve and mercy is the withholding of bad things we *do* deserve. Grace is something we live under 24/7 — it never ceases. Jesus was sent to earth to pay for our sins so that we would not get what we deserved for them. He also gave us access to something we didn't deserve. He took the eternal consequence for our imperfections so we could be in relationship with a perfect God.

In the last chapter, I explained how the law of bitter root judgments operates as taught by Elijah House Ministries International. The law of sowing and reaping suggests that when a bad tree is growing in our life, it is due to our judgements, which can also determine our future destiny (i.e. we reap what we sow). But James 2:13 says the law of mercy trumps the law of judgment. When I assist a client in identifying judgment and help them to forgive the people they judge/repent of their judgments, we make a spiritual movement towards uprooting the bad tree and making room for a new "judgment" or belief that aligns with God's word. The law of mercy then triumphs the law of judgement.

Jesus explicitly tells us how God will treat us if we don't forgive our brother or sister in the parable of the unmerciful servant (Matthew 18:21-35; refer to chapter five for the actual text). Theologically, I believe Jesus was talking about the law of judgments/sowing and reaping in this parable, not eternal salvation. I have yet to meet a person who doesn't have some measure of unforgiveness wedged against someone else or buried in their heart. I believe we all carry some level of resentment, bitterness, or unforgiveness, even if we are not aware of it. Remember, when we forgive, show mercy, and bless, we receive these things (forgiveness, mercy, and blessings) as well. This idea falls within the principle of "you get what you give," but because the law of grace and mercy trumps the law of judgment, we don't reap the consequence of our judgment eternally. Jesus created a hierarchy to ensure we don't always reap what we sow.

It says in many places in scripture (i.e. Proverbs 3:34; James 4:6; 1 Peter 5:5), "God opposes the proud but shows grace/favor to the humble." I believe these are the only places where God actually says he opposes us (and in Proverbs 16:18 where He says, "pride goes before a fall"). But in Proverbs 6:16-19, it says:

> [16] There are six things the LORD hates,
> seven that are detestable to him:
> [17] **haughty eyes, (pride)**
> a lying tongue, (**speaking curse, deceit, gossip/slander**)
> hands that shed innocent blood,
> [18] a heart that devises wicked schemes,
> feet that are quick to rush into evil,
> [19] a false witness who pours out lies, (**criticism, gossip, judgment**)

and a person who stirs up conflict in the community. (**gossip and judgment**).

Anytime we judge, criticize, curse, etc., we are operating in pride, but mercy and grace trump everything. Throughout the Word, God specifically reiterates that He is perfect, His love is perfect, and love trumps everything. Grace is love in action. I am not sure He leaves this entirely up to a universe of laws that we can see. Humility, then, seems to trump every other character quality. Humility is recognizing we will forever have a "log in our eye" because our imperfect human form, or ego, is bound in flesh. It also recognizes we will forever have the favor of a Father who loves us in a way we cannot earn or deserve. Humility allows us to believe and trust this Papa to give us what we ask for while not worrying about tomorrow. If we have favor from God for no particular reason (because we can't earn it), then we don't judge ourselves as having earned or deserved it. We don't deserve favor nor can we earn it, no matter how hard we try. We have favor simply because He wants to show us it as an act of His unconditional love. By its very definition, unconditional means we can't earn or lose it. All of these laws work together to prepare us for an atmosphere of high vibration.

The law of grace and mercy is an inexplicable law that has no formula. It says that sometimes you don't get consequences for your action because of God's decision to override the laws He set forth. There are many testimonies of people receiving miraculous grace directly from God. Here is an example of this...

When Tom was fourteen-years-old, he and his buddies were bored one night and decided to take his dad's car for a spin. Their ignorance and immaturity caused them to neglect to consider it was the middle of winter and the roads were covered in a thick layer of ice. Because of this, and their inexperienced driving, Tom ended up planting his dad's car on the neighbor's lawn. Tom came clean to his parents about the accident, but the neighbors pressed charges, forcing Tom to appear in court. Because he had broken several laws, the normal consequence for his actions would be that he would not be able to get his driver's lisence until he turned eighteen. At the time, Tom did not know the Lord personally, but inside, he wished for a miracle. He wished he would not suffer the consequence of his bad choices. Somehow, Tom's file was lost in the courtroom resulting in his case being dismissed. No one prayed for this to happen. No one begged God for mercy on Tom's behalf. No one even knew to do that. This incident can only be explained by God choosing to step in and override the normal process of justice, extending mercy to Tom.

Just like Tom, God gives us things we don't deserve daily and often when we have not known to ask for what we want according to the law of attraction. This is grace and it comes from a real, living, and personal savior and Holy Spirit, not an impersonal universe. I know people who don't seem to practice any of the laws mentioned and they still have favor in their lives in certain areas. I have heard many supernatural stories of angels appearing suddenly to protect in what seems to be a random situation. Other stories tell of some unsolicited miraculous intervention or turn of events to stop a devastation. It seems that sometimes God just randomly decides to give grace without explanation. Isn't that just like a loving dad to do?

Perhaps there is an order to the law of grace and mercy and maybe it is just too complex for our finite minds to comprehend. As I stated earlier, in the field of meteorology there is a principle called "the butterfly effect." The principle basically concludes that in the science of weather, the world is so intricately connected that if a butterfly in South America changes its flight pattern, it could eventually affect the weather in New York City. This is part of the science of chaos. Since God created the universe and the Earth (and thus the science of chaos), then it's not farfetched to think there might be some laws that are trumped without explanation. The law of grace and mercy is one of these exceptions. Throughout scripture, there are verses that explain the conditions man must follow to receive favor from God (not pertaining to eternal life). There seems to be no discernible criteria for why He chooses to gift and anoint certain people or rescue some from negative consequences while others still suffer. We can look at all the people in the Bible and wonder, "Why did God choose them?" He gives no explanation. It's all according to His plans and His purpose.

Tom had no explanation for why they lost the file. He wished for God to help him when he didn't even really know God. You could argue that Shadrach, Meshach, and Abednego should have burned. They didn't even ask God to let them live, but He chose to send Jesus into the fire and perform a miracle. It's hard to compare their story to those about Christian martyrs who were burned at the stake or those thrown into the coliseum to be eaten by lions. Why would God rescue three Hebrews from a fiery furnace but allow thousands of His followers to be persecuted and killed for their faith?

I have heard stories of people in Muslim countries who have had Jesus appear to them in dreams which caused them to give their life to Him. Why them and not every other person on Earth? I could recall numerous stories that prove God trumps His own laws sometimes, or again, He acts in accordance with an incredibly complex formula (science of chaos) that no human can unravel. Perhaps one of the keys to this "formula" has to do with the prayers of other people.

Quantum physics suggests we are all interconnected through an energetic grid or field. Prayer connects us to others instantly through intention. I don't believe we will fully understand the science of chaos related to God until we are in Heaven. I believe the principles of grace and mercy define the character of God and solidify that He views us as sons that sometimes just don't get what we deserve (John 3:16). The love of the Father trumps the law of sowing and reaping.

It is possible that the law of grace and mercy exists outside of the law of attraction, stacking the odds in our favor (lest we try to put God in a box). If the law of grace and mercy were not in place, we would always attract what our thoughts and feelings manifest. The cross is our assurance of this and promises that we will never be separated from the love of God. The Bible repeatedly talks about Christians as being "sons" and "co-heirs with Christ" (Romans 8:17) who are "seated in heavenly places" (Ephesians 2:6). We did not earn this position through attraction, it was a gift. By its very nature, a gift is not earned.

Would providing an avenue to raise our vibration in every circumstance not fit the characteristics of a loving God? Would God not want to elevate us to a higher place of peace and joy in every situation? When we can truly forgive and let go of judgment, we end up with greater insight into our own blind spots. When we experience grace, it enables us to have greater grace for others. If our purpose on Earth is to become more like Jesus through loving our enemies and neighbors like we do ourselves (Luke 6:27-35; Matthew 5:44), then every time we successfully apply forgiveness, grace, mercy, and blessing in the midst of a challenge, we raise our frequency, becoming a little more like Jesus. If we want to receive the law of grace and mercy instead of the law of sowing and reaping, we must extend grace and mercy to others.

Let me be clear, this process requires that we set and enforce healthy boundaries and understand that grace does not always mean there are no consequences to our actions. Forgiveness, blessing, grace, and mercy *can* coexist with expectations for your peers' behavior, the removal of toxic relationships, and the consequences of sin. The application of these principles is not your reluctant agreement to become a "doormat," but is an avenue of release from the bitterness and weight attached to being sinned against. Be encouraged and released from the idea that forgiveness does not always mean reconciliation of someone's behavior.

CHAPTER 9
WHAT IS THE HEART?
"As a man thinks in his heart, so is he."
Proverb 23:7

Earlier, I quoted Philippians 4:6-8 (NIV) which says:

> [6]Do not be anxious about anything, but in every situation, by prayer and petition, with thanksgiving, present your requests to God. [7]And the peace of God, which transcends all understanding, will guard your hearts and your minds in Christ Jesus. [8]Finally, brothers and sisters, whatever is true, whatever is noble, whatever is right, whatever is pure, whatever is lovely, whatever is admirable-if anything is excellent or praiseworthy-think about such things.

I wonder how many people let something go once they pray about it. In the practice of intercession, intercessors feel a burden to pray for a particular thing until they feel a release from the thing for which they are contending. You may be thinking, "But what about when the issue is personal?" How many of us pray about a need or a stress but then continue to worry about how God will take care of it?

I struggled with the issue of worrying for many years. I felt a heavy burden for my mother to accept Christ as her savior. In 1990, I went on a fast for this burden, to entreat God to move and assure me she would be saved. A few days into the fast, I heard an audible voice say, "It's a done deed." The burden lifted. I called my mom expecting to lead her to Christ, but it did not go well. A couple of years later, in an argument, I told her the Lord told me she would give her life to Christ, even though I had not yet seen it happen. Still, I never felt the burden return. A couple more years went by and she did finally give her life to Christ. She told me that for years she believed she had "grieved the Holy Spirit" at a younger age and wouldn't get another chance to receive Christ in her heart. She had spent her life staying busy to avoid thinking about what she thought was her certain eternal destiny: hell. She said when I told her God had told me she would find Christ, it gave her hope. It caused me deep agony that a misunderstood religious dogma had kept her from peace for so many years. I truly experienced Philippians 4:6 during this time in my life. Even though I had prayed about this issue for years, I continued to be anxious and fearful of the outcome. When the Holy Spirit spoke to my heart, I was never again anxious about this request.

One of the experiential difficulties in Philippians 4:6-8 lies in truly believing God hears and will answer. In *The Secret*, one contributor says that to enact the law of attraction, we have to think about what we want as if we are ordering from an online catalog. Once we "order" what we want, we must let it go and expect it to manifest. If we keep "ordering" it, then we don't truly believe we will receive it.[xlii] Other authors say we should repeatedly practice visualizing what we want and feeling as if we have received it. Some authors and teachers that specialize on the law of attraction believe there are contradictions about the effectiveness of this technique because it is more complicated than a simple formula. Perhaps the seeming contradiction is not factoring in the subconscious and its influence on our ability to believe.

The biggest challenge lies in the fact that we are only aware of about 5% of our thoughts and usually the anxiety lies in the 95% that is subconscious. (Some of that 95% is implicit memory, like how to lift a glass and drink, etc.) Our trapped emotions and experiences lead us to believe God is not trustworthy. Because of this, we believe God will not answer our prayers, or that we will suffer from an unwanted outcome. Later in the book, I will go into more detail about how trapped emotions create beliefs and how these govern our lives. But in spite of this subconscious influence, Paul tells us to embrace Philippians 4:6-8, praying on all things and being anxious for nothing.

This notion of only thinking positive thoughts may seem impossible. If I told people that I never think about anything bad or negative at all, they would most likely say, "You do not live in reality then," or " That is not practical. What about all the evil, pain, and suffering in the world?" But isn't this exactly what Paul is telling us to do in this scripture? If you believe the law of attraction to be true, then you must assess how much of your time is spent focusing on the positive, Philippians 4:8 type of things and be more aware of how much time you spend thinking about negative things. Remember there is no real distinction between prayer and thought if God is omniscient and omnipresent. The power is in your intention, not the words coming out of your mouth. When words do not resonate with belief, we are misaligned. If brain science tells us that our subconscious mind is up to 30,000 times more powerful than our conscious mind, imagine what results we would get when the two align.

Since we are only aware of about 5% of the thoughts we have each day, the rest of our 60,000-ish thoughts are subconscious.[xliii] We can make ourselves aware of some of them by paying attention, but most thoughts are automatic. We can call this part of our subconscious our "heart." Few people may learn to be more aware with practice, but ultimately, our subconscious is more powerful than our conscious.

Did you know the heart has an electromagnetic field 60-1000 times greater than the brain? It has almost as many memory cells as the brain. It also releases hormones like the brain. It can "think" for itself. The neurons in the heart enable it to learn, remember, and make decisions independent of the brain. Did you know the electromagnetic field of two people touching, or within a few feet of each other, can interact so that energy activity in the heart of one person is measured in the brain waves of the other?[xliv] In essence, one can "know another's heart" just by connecting energetically. When we carry physical, emotional, or spiritual wounds, we create energetic walls around our heart and reducing and/or compromising our heart connection with others. If we understand the electromagnetic pull of the heart and the law of attraction, it helps to form an image of how we attract what is in our heart. As our heart becomes free of negative energy, it emits and attracts a more positive energetic pull, magnetically drawing in what it desires. When it is weighted down with negative energy, it emits and attracts negative things. Joy, peace, and love attract positive things; fear, shame, guilt, and bitterness attract negative things. The heart field is a powerful magnet. We intuitively know this power as mankind has been obsessed with the heart for as long as we have been alive

History and language give us insight into this concept. How many words do we use every day that include the word "heart," "heartache," heartbreak," "know by heart," "in my heart," etc. We have been speaking for centuries about the idea that the heart thinks for itself. Even Proverbs 23:7 alludes to the heart having pervasive power over our thinking. It does not say, "As a man thinks in his mind," it says, "As a man thinks in his HEART," SO IS HE. Essentially what God is telling us is that our subconscious beliefs control our life. Many psychologists have known this to be true for years.

A fascinating area of research is that of heart transplants. The stories provide details given by those who have received hearts as a result of another person's death. You can find many of these stories on the internet. Some outcomes of the transplants have shown the following:

- Heart transplant recipients gained new likes and dislikes for certain types of food.
- Heart recipient's likes for activities such as shopping, musical instruments, and types of music changed.
- One man fell in love with the widow of the man who donated his heart due to suicide. The heart recipient and widow eventually married. Tragically, the recipient ended up committing suicide years later.
- A young girl received a heart from another young girl who was murdered. The heart recipient was able to identify the killer of the donor and where he lived from dreams she had after the transplant. The man confessed to killing the heart donor.

Many more of these amazing stories tell us that the heart holds keys to our identity and thoughts. These thoughts are controlled by:

- Our past experiences
- Our inherited beliefs
- Memories we develop before age 3-4 (when chronological memory begins)
- Our trapped emotions
- Beliefs that are formed from billions of experiences that we give meaning to
- Ancestral emotions and the beliefs handed down from our ancestor's experiences

I once had a client who sought me out for therapy after she had receivied a heart transplant five years earlier. In her case, the ghost of the original heart owner (a young man who was killed in a motorcycle accident) was attached to the heart she had received. This ghost (or soul body) named Justin would speak to this client and she could even feel him touching her hand. We followed a process developed by Arthur Burk to evict the ghost from her body.[xlv] Perhaps some of the other heart recipients mentioned were connected to the ghost of their heart donors through the heart's memory cells, like my client was to Justin.

One of the principles in scripture that is highly debated is the concept of soul ties. Soul ties are energetic or soul-based bonds/ties with another person that can be formed through trauma or sexual intercourse. When encouraging young people to practice abstinence, one of the supporting factors is that when we have sex with someone, we create a heart bond or soul tie. We give them a piece of our heart that may or may not be taken care of properly. If, over time, we give away too many pieces to too many people, metaphorically, we are operating on less than a whole heart. Energetically, we have many strings forever connecting us to those people, dulling and/ or compromising our light or magnetic heart energy. Very often, people with multiple soul ties never find true connections or happiness as long as those soul ties exist. Many of my clients who have a past filled with promiscuity, repeated failed relationships, and/or despair over still being single/divorced for many years will come to me disenchanted and struggling with a variety of issues.

In one case, I did a soul tie release with a woman who was married to her second husband for the past fifteen years, but had never disavowed the marriage vow to her first husband. In most marriage vows, we say, "I promise to _____ until death do us part" or "as long as we both shall live." When we get divorced, we legally end the tie, but not spiritually. The power from our vows, oaths, or promised words still hold us to that original bond of intention. When we disavowed this client's first marriage vow, we broke the soul tie with husband number one. In her next therapy session, she shared she had felt a new level of freedom. She also shared that in the past fifteen years, every time she went to fill out paperwork for husband number two, she would inadvertently write husband number one's social security number in the forms. After she broke the marriage vow and soul tie to husband number one, she reported that she completely forgot husband number one's social security number and never mistakenly wrote it on paperwork again.

In another case, I had a client who had lived with her (ex)boyfriend for two years. She reported that when they moved in together, she noticed her boyfriend would drink coffee every morning and a glass of wine every evening. Previously, this client had not done this, but she picked up this habit when they lived together. After they broke up, she continued the same daily habit. She told me that the very next day after we broke the soul tie between her and her boyfriend, she woke up and had lost her desire for coffee and wine.

The physical heart itself is charged with a massive amount of electromagnetic energy and has many memory cells and neuronal pathways. The subconscious is, at least in part, comprised of the heart (both structurally and energetically), as well as the brain and, in my opinion, the human spirit. We seem to connect the heart with our sense of conscience, including our good intentions towards others, but also our bad intentions. Our heart remembers everything and every connection it has made. We do not fully know this iceberg nor can we. We cannot monitor every thought, know every source of our beliefs, every memory, nor can we stop every painful emotion. We can choose to keep a wall around our heart and block its beautiful energy from truly connecting with someone else's or we can learn to feel, process, and release negative emotions and traumas, look for and connect with other people who are connected to their hearts, and live powerful transformational lives.

God loves us and His word is designed to give us truth that helps us to become most aligned with our highest good. If we truly understand and believe, "As a man thinks in his heart, so is he," then giving our heart away to too many people or having many unresolved relationships greatly affects the things we think in our heart. If we become what we think in our heart, then those whom we have connected with on a heart level can greatly affect our vibration, frequency, and ultimately, how our life looks.

CHAPTER 10
THE IMPACT OF
GENERATIONAL INIQUITY

In working in inner healing and deliverance for decades and now in energy medicine, I have observed consistent evidence that what our ancestors pass down to us has impact on our body, soul, and spirit. This is validated by scripture, genetic science, and evidence from case studies done through many professions. In a nutshell, the unresolved negative energies, as well as the positive energies, are passed down from ancestors to their descendants. These energies precede experience and can influence subconscious beliefs in the descendent. Most of an individuals' beliefs are created or programmed from the womb experience forward, but ancestral beliefs can influence the lenses through which an individual sees and experiences the world, even from very early in their life.

Everyone's DNA code has predispositions of traits, beliefs, and behaviors. The scriptures regarding generational iniquity are debated:

Exodus 20:5 (21st Century King James Version) says:
Thou shalt not bow down thyself to them, nor serve them: for I the LORD thy God am a jealous God, visiting the iniquity of the fathers upon the children unto the third and fourth generation of them that hate me...

But then Ezekiel 18:20 (ESV) says:
The soul who sins shall die. The son shall not suffer for the iniquity of the father, nor the father suffer for the iniquity of the son. The righteousness of the righteous shall be upon himself, and the wickedness of the wicked shall be upon himself.

While these seem contradictory, I believe the distinction is in actual punishment, not generational consequences. In the Old Testament, children were actually stoned or punished for their parents' sins. Achan hid silver from Jericho after Joshua made explicit instructions for everything to be dedicated as an offering and destroyed (it was accursed). After the Israelistes lost the battle of Ai, Joshua heard there had been disobedience in his instructions to destroy all artifacts from Jericho. Their law required that not only Achan, but his whole family be stoned for this act of disobedience (Joshua 7). Harsh! The spiritual iniquity principle claimed that taking the cursed object opened a door in the spirit realm for Satan to bring destruction to Israel. The disobedience was legal ground for the enemy to bring destruction. Because the Israelites believed iniquity could be passed down generationally, and that Achan's sin affected the whole nation, they believed his entire family must be destroyed in order to restore purity. In Exodus, the idea is that the sin of idolatry (worshipping another god) would carry an iniquity down generationally, but this was meant to be a spiritual effect, not a literal generational punishment.

Science will always line up with scripture because the creator of the universe is a God of order. The confusion lies in the idea that "Jesus became a curse for us to free us from the curse" (Galatians 3:13). So if "generational curses" were taken care of at the cross, why do we still see these occurring? Well, like everything related to the cross, we have to use the principle of appropriation. This principle says we must appropriate the blood of Jesus to the iniquities of our ancestors where they failed to do so. It is a process that is not automatically executed at salvation.

Epigenetics is the science of how and why genes are turned on or off in subsequent generations. Unresolved trauma and inherited experiences can change the genetic expressions of DNA based on environmental influences and even mental/emotional factors.[xlvi] Research shows how traits are passed down in potentiality form in the DNA. (They may or may not get turned on.) The principle of appropriation must be applied. Beliefs and thoughts must be changed intentionally. Contrary to popular belief, we don't get an automatic "everything is healed" when we accept

Christ. We are given a spiritual guarantee of Heaven, but our soul and body are still affected by the laws of the universe. If our ancestors were in rebellion to God and did not repent (change their mind), then those thoughts and deeds imprinted on their DNA are passed down, creating a potential negative energy in the lives of their descendants. The good news is that just because this negative energy exists does not mean we have to carry it. We have the ability to apply the blood of the cross and repent for our ancestors' sins, changing the manifestation of the DNA.

Science has shown our thoughts rewire our DNA.[xlvii] Most inner healing authorities agree that this principle is true. Just like appropriating our authority in Christ, we have to appropriate the closing of doors to our ancestors' iniquities in order to cut off any way the enemy can access our energy (typically through demonic strongholds and influences). I cannot stress enough that *this is not a curse from God*, but legal ground for the enemy to continue to torment the descendants of those who committed the original sin/iniquity. (There is a distinction between sin and iniquity. Sin means "to miss the mark or fall short." Iniquity refers to "repeated patterns of sin/strongholds/habits.") In recent years, much has been written on the concepts of the "courts of heaven" and legal ground.[xlviii] Elijah House Ministries has been teaching this principle for years. God follows the laws he set forth and Satan is a legalist who looks for the loopholes that will open doors to generational curses and destruction. Appropriation of the blood of Jesus and His grace is within our authority, but we have to actually practice it.

When interviewing other inner healers and ministers, I have found that sin and stronghold patterns are handed down in family lines. Biological science tells us that traits are handed down genetically through DNA, so it would not be a stretch to believe that what ancestors do impacts their descendants in some capacity. The principle of sowing and reaping is a framework for how this works in matters of spirit, soul, and body.

Several years ago, a study was carried out at Emory University to test if the trauma passed down in DNA could be measured. In this study, they:

...exposed mice to a cherry blossom scent and gave them elec-
tric foot shocks, so that the animals learned to associate the
scent with the fear of being shocked. Other mice were exposed
to a neutral scent or no scent.

The mice were allowed to mate, and their offspring were ex-
posed to varying amounts of the cherry scent. Those mice were
also allowed to mate, and their own offspring were exposed to
the scent as well.

The first-generation offspring were more sensitive to the cher-
ry scent — they could detect the scent at very low levels and
avoided spending a lot of time near the odor. What's more, the
next generation of offspring showed the same odor sensitivity,
according to results of the study.

The researchers also measured how the scent fear affected
brain anatomy, using a method that dyes odor neurons blue.
They counted these blue neurons and traced their origin.

The first- and second-generation offspring of the mice trained
to fear the cherry scent had greater amounts of a known chem-
ical receptor for the cherry blossom odor than offspring of mice
exposed to a neutral scent, and also had enlarged brain areas
devoted to those receptors.

In fact, even mice conceived from the sperm of a cherry
odor-fearing mouse displayed the same sensitivity to the scent,
the researchers found, suggesting the scent knowledge wasn't
something the mice learned from their parents.[xlix]

So, the descendants of those who were shocked when exposed to the smell of cherry blossoms were born with a fear triggered by the smell of cherry blossoms. We call this an epigenetic mutation.

When a traumatic event occurs, the amygdala will send information to the brain to develop a protective mechanism for future safety. This can lead to PTSD in extreme cases and, in less severe cases, hypervigilance. For example, if I was bitten by a dog (even at a young age), I may find myself nervous around dogs for the rest of my life. My brain has learned to associate dogs with pain, even if it is only my subconscious remembering the trauma and negative energy from the original event. If I never learn to like dogs, my subconscious will decide dogs are unsafe and promote a fearful response whenever I encounter them. This would be considered an epigenetic mutation that could be passed down to future generations.

Scientific studies have shown that our brain cannot determine the difference between something fully imagined and something experienced. The same neurons fire in both situations.[i] In other words, when our mind is focused on a perceived reality and fully engaged in our senses and emotions, our brain experiences this as real. So, if I am experiencing a virtual reality roller coaster ride, the same parts of my brain are going to fire as if I was on an actual roller coaster. What we believe creates our reality.

I once had a client who had a fear of flying present itself in her twenties. While working on identifying and releasing her fear of airplanes and flying, we found memories of scary flights she had experienced when she was younger. Because of her energy issues, flying and traveling often compromised her sleep and energy. (Electromagnetic radiation is heavy in airplanes and can impact those who are sensitive to electromagnetic frequencies.) Once we released all these issues, her anxiety when flying got a little better, but airplanes and flying still brought on an irrational fear.

In her earlier counseling sessions, I did not have the tools to identify generational trauma. One day, she was planning a trip and wanted to work on releasing her fear of flying in preparation. She told me she couldn't shake this idea that her fear had some connection with her father and his fearing that planes were faulty or unsafe. I immediately recognized something that had not occurred to me before. I asked her if her two siblings were also afraid of flying and she responded with a nod. All three children were afraid of flying. I used Applied Kinesiology (muscle testing) to see if her fear of flying was rooted in something generational, specifically from her father. She tested "yes". She mentioned she thought her dad may have been in the Air Force before he married her mother. Her father had passed away, but her mother was still alive. We released the trauma roots of knowing she inherited fear from her father, but I still encouraged her to ask her mother what she knew.

When we met for her next session, she couldn't wait to tell me what she had found out. It turned out her father had been a pilot in the Air Force and his job was to fly experimental planes. All of his squad had died in plane crashes due to faulty planes. Every time he got on a plane, it was like playing Russian roulette. He had developed a terror of flying because his life was literally at risk every time he boarded a plane. We released the stored energy from generational trauma that was occurring to her and she noticed a dramatic reduction in her fear of flying. Now, she has much more peace about boarding planes and being in the air.

Mark Wolynn, author of *It Didn't Start with You: How Inherited Family Trauma Shapes Who We Are and How to End the Cycle*, focuses his practice on finding and bringing relief to generational trauma. His research explains how trauma triggers epigenetic mutations in DNA and, like my practice, has found that symptoms and illnesses are inherited and directly related to specific traumas from previous generations. One of his examples describes a teenage girl who continually cut herself due to a ruminating belief that she "didn't deserve to live." Mark was able to identify that her grandmother had been in a car accident in which she was driving and was at fault for the death of her husband. He bled out at the scene of the accident due to cuts from shattered glass. The grandmother never spoke about this to anyone nor sought out any therapy, silently suffering from the trauma and guilt. Two generations later, her descendant was deeply afflicted with compulsions to cut herself with glass.[li]

Freemasonry and Patterns of Generational Iniquity

Recently, there has been increasing exposure of secret societies, their rituals, and intentions/origins. Whistleblowers, who were former members of these cults, have come forward to share intimate details of the secret rituals, oaths, and vows taken by those involved in these organizations. Let me give you a brief summary of how these organizations, particularly Freemasons and their connected organizations, fit into this model of generational iniquity. I am in no way accusing those involved in secret organizations of knowingly being Satanists/Luciferians or realizing they are part of a cult, but I am attempting to convey the effects of alignment, oaths, and vows.

At the outset of joining Freemasonry, a candidate must agree to forego their religious bias for the fraternal organization. The candidate must make a vow that no matter what goes on in the organization, they will never reveal what they have seen or heard. Making vows of secrecy rarely has a good outcome.

Jesus said in Matthew 5:33-37 (NIV):
"[33]Again, you have heard that it was said to the people long ago, 'Do not break your oath, but fulfill to the Lord the vows you have made.' [34] But I tell you, do not swear an oath at all: either by heaven, for it is God's throne; [35] or by the earth, for it is his footstool; or by Jerusalem, for it is the city of the Great King. [36]And do not swear by your head, for you cannot make even one hair white or black. [37]All you need to say is simply 'Yes' or 'No'; anything beyond this comes from the evil one."

James 5:12 (AMP) says:
But above all, my fellow believers, do not swear, either by heaven or by earth or with any other oath; but let your yes be [a truthful] yes, and your no be [a truthful] no, so that you may not fall under judgment.

Why would Jesus go out of His way to make sure His followers knew not to make oaths or vows? The law required them, but is He saying they are evil? Perhaps He recognized that when we make a vow we can't keep, we give the enemy legal ground to afflict us, especially in the area of the vow we took. If this is the truth, then it is imperative we grasp the seriousness of making oaths to any organization, especially ones that are secretly to a Satanic/Luciferian religion or that have the agenda of controlling and destroying their members' lives.

1 Peter 5:8 (NASB) says:
Be of sober spirit, be on the alert. Your adversary, the devil, prowls around like **a roaring lion**, seeking someone to devour.

John 10:10 (ESV) says:
The thief comes only to **steal and kill and destroy**; I came that they may have life and have it abundantly.

The thief (Satan) must have legal ground to devour, steal, kill, and destroy. If our ancestors make oaths to Satan, they give him permission to devour the blessings God has for their descendants, stealing their inheritance. Our ancestors may unknowingly open the doors for these afflictions to carry down through their generational line.

When Jesus healed blind Bartimaeus, he called Bartimaeus the "son of Timaeus" (Mark 10:46-52). Timaeus means "idol worshipper." There is a belief that blindness, deafness, and being mute comes from worshipping idols. (Idols are blind, deaf, and dumb.) Many deliverance experts will agree they have found these correlations. Jesus was pointing to the man's blindness as a result of idolatry. In Deuteronomy 28:15-16, we see the specific consequences of idol worship. According to this passage, worshipping idols gives the enemy permission to afflict us and when we don't turn away, it can have a generational effect.

The following are some of the actual elements (which are highly edited) contained in the Freemasonry renunciation prayer used to break ties with Freemasonry (whether they be personal or ancestral). The prayer, which was created by Selwyn Stevens of Jubilee Ministries, utilizes the actual wording from the thirty-three degrees a Freemason goes through to reach the highest level of the organization. Just from committing to the organization, they unwittingly vow to keep all the oaths (many of which are graphic and violent), opening themselves to the consequences of oaths they may have never sworn themselves. The prayer begins with "In the name of Jesus Christ, I renounce the oaths taken and the curses involved in…"

- Spirit, emotions, and eyes (including all confusion); fear of the dark, fear of the light, and fear of sudden noises
- Blinding of spiritual truth, the darkness of soul, the false imagination, condescension, the spirit of poverty, the usurping of the marriage covenant by the removal of the wedding ring
- The fear of choking and also every spirit causing asthma, hay fever, emphysema, or any other breathing difficulty; the fear of death by stabbing pain; the fear of heart attack from this degree
- Pride (resulting self-righteousness of being good enough to stand before God without the need of a savior); healing of the speech area including the throat, vocal chords, nasal passages, sinus, bronchial tubes, etc.; the curses on the heart and chest
- The curses on the stomach and womb area
- Spirit of death from the blows to the head; the fear of death, false martyrdom; fear of violent gang attack, assault or rape
- All fear of insanity, anguish, death wishes, suicide and death, anger, hatred, murderous thoughts, revenge, retaliation, spiritual apathy, false religion, all unbelief (especially unbelief in the Holy Bible as God's Word), all spiritual searching into false religions, and all striving to please God; healing of the brain, the mind, etc.
- Senses of smell and hearing being removed; of having the hands cut; the curse of bankruptcy that comes "ill fortune" over finances; "to pluck with violence" over finances, inheritance in Christ, and spiritual life; the stripping of all moneys to symbolize poverty; the curse of losing the home through bankruptcy, poverty and inability to secure a loan; all bondage of moving financially two steps forward, then three steps backwards or even one step backward; curse of the Poor Box of Freemasonry towards ungodly giving away of assets and blessings[lii]

Wow, that's a lot of curses that will affect the members of the secret society and their descendants if they leave, disagree, or reveal the secrets of the brotherhood. In my experience with clients who have Freemason ancestors, I have seen many of these physical issues manifested in their lives. Many former Freemasons concur with the same experiences. Clearly Stephens, who wrote this prayer, was aware of these same effects. The following are some the generational effects I have observed in the descendants of Freemasons.

Mental Illness/Chemical Imbalance

There is an epidemic of anxiety, depression, and other chemical imbalances in the United States. (While I don't classify a chemical imbalance as a mental illness, it certainly has the potential to become one.) In witchcraft, people use techniques to "open their third eye" in order to "see" in the spirit realm. This is giving permission to darkness we would otherwise not be accessing. From an energetic view, we can see what is passed down:

- The negative energy of keeping secrets
- Possible trauma kept secret
- Being afflicted by low frequency entities because of opening doors to them unknowingly

I have observed patterns of suicidal thoughts and attempts (which can be from a demonic spirit) in families that have Freemasonry in their ancestry. Not everyone struggling with depression and anxiety become suicidal; however, in my experience, in families where ancestors (often more than one) have taken their life, there is typically someone who participated in Freemasonry in the family trees. We can see the same lines drawn between alcoholism and other addiction in family trees. Alcohol and drugs are used to self-manage the chemical imbalances of depression and anxiety. The brain is driven to return to homeostasis or balance.

Studies have revealed an exponential increase in the occurrence of an epigenetic (environmentally changed) mutation called MTHFR which affects the body's ability to detox and uptake certain nutrients. People with MTHFR cannot properly process folic acid and vitamin B12, making them more likely to suffer from depression, anxiety, ADD, ADHD, adrenal, thyroid (and other glands), and hormonal issues because of malnutrition. Researchers cannot identify what caused this mutation—only that it is manifesting in increasing numbers.[liii] More than 60% of my clients require a methyl B product and report immediate changes in mood with consistent use. I have found a strong correlation between a methylation B issue and Freemasonry. I believe the participation in Freemasonry opens the door to a MTHFR mutation, thus, opening the door to mental illness, depression, thyroid problems, and other physical issues.

I can only draw this conclusion based on the correlation of my clients who need a methyl b product and also have Freemasonry in their family lineage. The DNA is somehow altered by the oaths and vows. We have discussed how the power of emotion and thought can alter DNA, so based on these conclusions, it makes sense that oaths and vows could alter DNA, especially in areas where traumas have occurred, secret vows have been kept, and consciences were afflicted in some way. Secrets, in my opinion, are never a good idea. In addiction recovery, we say: "Secrets make us sick."[liv]

Perhaps the person who has vowed in secrecy to Lucifer, even unknowingly (the subconscious knows all), lives in hidden despair which causes negative energy to effect the DNA. Again, I also believe the intention of the enemy is destruction, so the DNA is damaged by an open door or legal ground. If oaths and vows can alter the DNA energetically and allow for generational open doors, spiritually and/or physically, then Satan, the roaring lion seeking to whom he may devour (1 Peter 5:8) and whose plan is to steal, kill, and destroy (John 10:10), has the legal right to afflict the descendants.

Physical Illness and Unexplained Types of Autoimmune Diseases/Non-Pathogen Diseases

One of the Freemason rituals is a noose around the neck and curses on lungs, gut, and heart. Many researchers have found that one of the energetic roots of autoimmune disease is self-hatred.[iv] As I accumulate negative energy against myself (in the form of emotions, thoughts, sins against my conscience, and alignments with negative sources), I can create disease within my own body. Remember Dr. Emoto's experiments? Freemasons know in their heart they have made agreements to accept disease and physical bodily destruction.

Early on in my experience with clients who had Freemasonry in their ancestry, I had a new client with multiple autoimmune and gastrointestinal issues. At the beginning of her therapy, I prayed we would find some real roots immediately. The very first thing I tested was Freemasonry. She recalled her uncle talking to her dad about it. Her father and grandfather were the founders of a Christian commune that operated more like a cult. The children went to work at a young age, had little contact with their parents, and experienced little joy, love, or affirmation. They had been programmed to believe God was a cruel master, always ready to punish. My client and her husband had left the cult several years prior to our sessions. This was a very difficult decision for them to make as it is hard to escape cult environments. After our first session, I sent her the Freemason prayer. At our next session, she told me that prior to reading the prayer she would have the same recurring dream. The dream went like this:

> We are taking the children to visit my grandfather for the weekend. (He was head over the farm where they lived as adults in the cult.) At the end of the weekend, we go to leave and realize we are stuck there. Trapped. we can't leave. When I wake up from the dream, I am so relieved I literally hug my bed.

When we did a dream interpretation, we found two common elements. First, a house usually represents a life. This is her grandfather's house. Second, dreaming of an ancestor usually points to something we inherited in that family line. So, she was trapped by something from her grandfather's life (Freemasonry). She told me that after she prayed the prayer, that same night she had this dream:

The dream is exactly the same except that at the end of the weekend we simply load up the car and leave.

The renunciation prayer freed her from being trapped by her grandfather's inherited iniquities. She has since healed of the autoimmune diseases and her traumatic childhood and now practices as a holistic energy healer. This is just one example of many where I have found thyroid issues, asthma, lung, heart and stomach issues that were seemingly unexplained, but later found them to be linked to Freemasonry.

Feeling and Belief of Superiority (Narcissism)

Freemasonry is linked to the Illuminati. The Illuminati believe they are direct descendants of Lucifer and therefore both "god" and human, thus superior to humans. This belief is infused all throughout Freemasonry. We have had a seeming epidemic of narcissistic abuse in the past few years. Many of my clients have been married to narcissists and report their husbands suffer from an unrealistic self-opinion. Grandiosity is one of many traits of a narcissist, but they do not see that in themselves and lack self-awareness in general. Also, many Freemasons are successful businessmen, doctors, lawyers, and professionals which breeds self-righteousness (as in the prayer). A descendant may not necessarily know why they feel superior, they just do. It may not line up with their accomplishments in the natural world, but they carry a sense of being more enlightened and superior to everyone else, even those of advanced position. (Illuminati means "enlightened ones.")

Some Form of Sexually Destructive Behavior or Vulnerability

I have had many cases where a client has been sexually abused or molested and with some examining, I find it is also occurring in more than one family member and that these family members have ancestral ties to Freemasonry. The same is true for incest, pornography, homosexuality, and infidelity. Freemasonry opens the door for current and future family members to struggle with sex acts shrouded in destruction and defilement.

All the way back to Babylon, the Illuminati have needed sexual energy to thrive and elevate evil powers. Rituals always involved the rape of children, orgies, and other sexual acts (as well as blood acts) because they believed it to bring greater power. Every occultic religion has ritually used pedophilia and sex as part of their worship. Satanists (i.e. the Illuminati and the origins of Freemasonry) practice these rituals currently:

- Sexual abuse: This is always found generationally in families. People with this iniquity will attract predators. There is a spiritual or energetic attraction. A predator will find the kid who has this generational iniquity and abuse them. It is magnetic and subconscious. Descendants of Freemasons/the Illuminati inherit this open door to sexual violation. Satanists will offer up their and other's children to the coven for sexual violation.
- Incest: The sexual abuse of children by parents/family members correlates to descendants of Freemasons and occult-involved generational lines. It is often programmed as "normal" within the family system.
- Perversion: Descendants will inherit lust, sexual appetites, and a sex drive that may be exaggerated and open to vulgar and profane practices. This may include homosexuality and other deviant sexual behavior. Descendants may be highly sexual even if they were not abused (although a large percentage will be abuse victims). The programming they may have inherited is considered very sexual (women are sex slaves and men are predators).

There is a spirit, a power that the descendants of Freemasonry/the Illuminati can inherit. It feels powerful (like the superiority feeling) and they know they have influence over people — changing their minds, dictating what they do, and converting their thinking. They can easily control and manipulate people to get whatever they want. Some use this power for the kingdom (i.e. persuading people to go to church or accept Jesus), but the power is a counterfeit for the Holy Spirit's anointing and not from God. (God can redeem it, but they have to realize its occult origins and let it go first.) They make good salesmen and compelling motivational speakers, but they are robbed of peace and consumed by a fear of what will happen if they lose this power. The fear that God may take away their power influences legalism and performance. This power strip could mean financial loss, loss of followers, and loss of influence — much of what their identity or esteem is built on. This is why they lack peace. Their very identity is built on sinking sand.

The spirit behind this false anointing comes from fallen angelic DNA (when fallen angels bred with humans, as it says in Genesis 6:1-5). This demonic, angelic, sexual covenant opened the door for men to have access to a greater measure of soul power. This is the kind of power that Adam walked in before he and Eve were deceived. Descendants of Freemasons may inherit greater soul power, which can be used in various manners. Many times, they are convinced that because they are Freemasons, they will have favor in business because members support and promote each other (Good Ol' Boy's Club). Often, they do succeed, so they essentially believe their favor comes from Freemasonry (idolatry) and not from God.

In energy theory, a miasm is a negative vibrational health issue that is passed down generationally from one or both parents to children. It is a predisposition to struggle with certain issues that is activated by stress, not a definitive genetic defect in the DNA. It is not widely known in western medicine, but is effectively remedied with vibrational therapies.[lvi] The DNA is more like a tuning fork than a predetermined set of facts, so things can be changed by vibration.

106

Do you know if there is ancestral Freemasonry in your family?

Do you recognize any of these ancestral iniquities in your family? Chances are, you have these open doors in your life.

Double Binds

One of the principles of sickness in energy medicine and holistic thought is the idea of double binds. A double bind is a lose-lose situation. I like to say it's the ping pong match in your head. You can't decide because both choices will result in loss or pain, so you keep debating and ruminating over what to do. From an energetic standpoint, this is a constant state of fear and worry in the subconscious. From what you have already learned, imagine the amount of negative energy that has accumulated in a double bind. Mental, emotional, and physical symptoms can result from being stuck in double binds. Much of the work I do is identifying double binds in the client's thinking. By showing them where they created a faulty or destructive belief, I can help them to reprogram it. You can never achieve true peace and joy while battling double binds.

In Freemasonry, there is most likely a point where the member hits a double bind. They realize there is something dark or off about the organization they are involved in, but are afraid of "leaving the cult." (This is true in all occult organizations.) They have been led to believe bad things will happen (as stated in the vows and oaths) if they break fellowship and leave, so they feel stuck and trapped. Even worse, if there is any ritual involvement at any point that is illegal, they are also trapped legally. Every criminal has this same issue; they either stay and violate their conscience or face the potentially life-threatening consequences of leaving. In Freemasonry, they might be ostracized or lose money/business when facing the consequences of the vows.

A client of mine shared the story of how this double bind affected his father, who was a 33rd degree Freemason, the highest attainable level. Three weeks after accepting Christ as his Lord and Savior, the client's father died in a car accident. One of the consequences of breaking the oaths of Freemasonry is that the member will experience curses, physical ailments, and death — consequences similar to many other occult groups and gangs. The ex-Freemason was unaware that he must repent of the oaths that were made when he joined the organization or else he would experience the curses invoked in those oaths (remember Matthew 5:33-37). Because he did not have the proper guidance in renouncing the oaths he made in Freemasonry, he suffered the consequences of trying to leave the group.

Sadly, he did not appropriate the level of renunciations needed to close all the doors to iniquities in his family line. Many will acknowledge Freemasonry's effect and pray a prayer of repentence but will fail to actively seek measures to destroy the personal and ancestral ties they have made with the organization. These actions must then be remedied by the descendants through the principle of appropriation in order to free their family line from generational bondage.

CHAPTER 11
THE IMPACT OF TRAPPED EMOTIONS AND THE MEANING WE GIVE THEM

Muscle testing shows us that trapped emotions can be stored in our heart from conception. The fetus in the womb absorbs emotions from its mother. Babies and young children absorb emotions experienced in their family environment. We can absorb other people's emotions that then become trapped in us at any given time. These negative balls of energy can be stored in any part of our body. Dogs often absorb their master's emotions. Parents experience intense feelings from their children's experiences that can then become trapped in them. Therapists and ministers know they must debrief and process the empathy they experience for clients who share intense emotions.

Often many churches use the scripture Philippians 3:13, "forgetting what is behind," to tell us that inner healing or dealing with family origin issues is not Biblical. Those in the therapy and inner healing realm know that our current perceptions and intentions for the future are dictated by our subconscious beliefs. These beliefs are formed by our life experiences and the perceptions/conclusions we drawn from those experiences. Our past dictates our future by default, unless we override it.

The more intensely emotional or traumatic an experience is for us, the more likely there will be negative belief systems formed by it and corresponding trapped emotions. Trapped emotions are physical balls of low vibration energy that reside in our hearts and other parts of our bodies. We all have them in abundance. Whenever an event happens, our response will be first out of our heart. Thus, our initial reaction will be based on the past experiences, subconscious beliefs, and trapped emotions that are triggered by how the event "occurs" to us or how we perceive it. Nothing really occurs objectively; it is taken into the brain after being filtered by the heart and the amygdala (the trauma center of the brain). We are then responsible for the meaning.

The experiences of our past shape what we believe from the time we are born until the time we die. Quantum physics, energy medicine, and inner healing documentations tell us that some of our memories are formed even before birth. Science has determined that trauma and continued thought have the power to change DNA itself.[lvii] This is another backing to Dr. Emoto's water study. Our heart is not only affected by our own negative experiences, but potentially by the negative experiences of our ancestors. "As a man thinks" is passed down in the DNA.

We have learned we can inherit trauma and beliefs from our ancestors and that we absorb energy in the womb, from our surroundings, and from our parents, but much of who we are is made from the meanings we apply to our given situations. Let's say I am five-years-old at my first day of kindergarten. I have no siblings and have been kept from playing with other children. I move to a new community (uprooting is stressful) and start school. At recess, the kids surround me and begin to bully me by calling me names. I am feeling humiliated, rejected, overwhelmed, and fearful, but have no words to identify these emotions. I start to cry. The teacher sees me. She comes over, puts her arm around me, comforts me, and then asks why I am crying. I tell her the kids are making fun of me. She scolds them, tells them to apologize, and to treat their new classmate nicely. She reminds them how important kindness is. They apologize and we go off and play together. In this situation, I would have felt heard, been comforted, my emotions would have been validated, I received an apology, and all issues were reconciled.

Well, in most cases that is a fairy tale. In reality, when I started to cry, the kids would most likely make fun of me more. The teacher may never intervene in the situation; she either doesn't see the conflict or believes we should work it out ourselves. I would go back to class like a deer in headlights. When I go home and my mother asks me how my day was, I will give her one of two answers. I will either say "fine" because I have already learned to believe mom is not safe, or I will start to cry, and mom will ask what happened and I will tell her. She will probably tell me that kids can be mean and I have to learn how to not be so sensitive. Either way, I have not had a place to express and process all the emotions I felt during the conflict.

I would have to go back to school the next day and at recess, it would most likely happen again. Now, I will start to give their behavior meaning. While feeling rejected, I will decide something must be wrong with me since they are not making fun of anyone else. While feeling scared, I will decide kids are mean and can't be trusted. In feeling unprotected, I will decide school is an unsafe place. In states of heightened emotion, we make decisions about ourselves, others, and bigger things like life, school, work, parents, God, church, sports, etc. These beliefs feel VERY true because of the strength of the unprocessed emotions behind them. The emotions are the concrete holding the blocks of beliefs in place and making them feel true each time I am in a situation where I feel these emotions again.

Joe Dispenza teaches that emotion is primarily magnetic and thought is primarily electrical. When you put them together, you form an electromagnetic bond which acts like a magnet.[lviii] Like attracts like. What you believe is an electromagnetic force and becomes a magnet. So, you attract what you believe to be true. In this case of five-year-old me, I will continue to attract people who are mean and reject me, and I will continue to believe that school is an unsafe place. The original belief created in that state of heightened emotion will send out electromagnetic waves that will attract the same frequency. I repeatedly experience this belief as true. This becomes my reality and then I walk around, subconsciously attracting what I expect. It is not a universal truth like 2 + 2; however, because it was made in a state of heightened emotion, it is concrete to me and is actually bonded together in my subconscious. What I believe in my subconscious reality manifests in my conscious reality. "As a man thinks...." This is called faith. I manifest what my faith puts energy into.

As mentioned before, muscle testing (Applied Kinesiology) has been practiced for several decades and been proven valid in thousands of experiments. Muscle testing is an energy process. When our vibration changes, our physical strength changes as well. There are many commonly used and effective applications of muscle testing. Allergists find allergies by holding substances up to your body and if your muscles go weak, then that substance affects you adversely. Chiropractors find the specific vertebrae in your body that are out of alignment (called subluxations) because these places throw off your energetic circuits. Natural practitioners find infections and organ stress that contributes to slowing down your energetic circuits. The science behind lie detector tests tells us that when we make a false statement, the energy flow in our body changes and we emit a different vibration.

Did you know that a belief, trauma, or trapped emotion that occurred before the age of four can be triggered by something in the present? The triggered emotions will feel as if the offense that happened long ago is happening right now because of the hippocampus, the part of the brain that stores chronological memory. It develops between ages three and four. Before then, our memories are more like snapshots that have feelings and sensory stimulus attached to them (smell, touch, etc.). Thus, it is harder to identify original trauma when it is triggered by a current event if the root belief was established before the age of three. What this means in terms of the law of attraction is that much of what we experience in life (manifestation) is determined by the vibration we create from these beliefs in our heart. "As a man thinks...."

Teachers of the law of attraction make it seem easy to attract all the good things. The law says that good outweighs bad by a great deal. Some proponents believe that if 10-20% of our conscious and subconscious beliefs are positive, they will outweigh the negative and our heart's desires will be communicated to the universe. I can't verify the percentage that has to be positive, but I can validate that as we release negative emotions and beliefs, replacing them with positive emotions and beliefs, we begin to attract things and situations that are more positive because our vibration changes.

By applying Philippians 4:8 (think on good things) and 2 Corinthians 10:5 (take thoughts captive) to our conscious thoughts, and James 3:9-10 (bless don't curse) to our words, we could make great strides in changing our vibration. This requires the discipline of focusing our attention on what we are thinking and saying. It also requires us to perform the difficult actions in the scriptures mentioned above. This is not an automatic process, but one that has to be done with deliberation. There are many practical ways to achieve this, which will be discussed in a later chapter; however, the main point is that we *must* release the negative emotions. These are actual balls of trapped negative energy inside us. Motivational speakers who touch on the law of attraction often miss this part and have a low percentage of successful outcomes from their seminars. Emotions are the glue or concrete that imprison negative beliefs. You can't successfully reprogram your beliefs while strong, negative emotions continue to make them feel true.

Think of your life like a big bowl filled with tiny balls of energy. All the experiences in your life where you did not get to process negative thoughts and feelings are included. Most Americans may say they feel very disconnected due to bowls full of unprocessed negative emotions. Many may have never felt they were in a safe environment to process their negative emotions because they were taught that showing emotion is a sign of weakness or emotions are evil/bad. The church is especially notorious for villainizing God-given emotions. We (including the church) are the most addicted, depressed, anxious, obese, medicated, and sick nation in the world, so perhaps the things we have been practicing aren't working so well. What do you think?

Remember the iceberg metaphor? 95% of our thoughts are subconscious and 5% of our thoughts are conscious. Changing the 95% requires deliberate effort. Seeking out healing for our traumas, releasing trapped emotions, and utilizing other techniques to access our subconscious, can result in noticeable changes in our thoughts, feelings, and behaviors. Again, this process is not easy, but it provides worthwhile transformation in our heart, soul, mind, and spirit.

We are body, soul, and spirit joined together. There is not a specific delineation between these parts of man. Any changes we make in one area will affect the others as well. Nothing that occurs to us is purely spiritual, physical, or soulish (mind, will, and emotions). Energy theory believes that all physical pain and issues (with the exception of direct impact trauma or misalignment) are rooted in emotional, spiritual, or other energetic caus-es. The AMA agrees that 90% of disease has emotional or mental roots (and yet they don't train doctors with this in mind). If we understand the body, soul, and spirit are energy/atomic structures with various vibrations, then there is a multidimensional cause for every issue. This is the premise for holistic health. For example, if a client is battling depression, they are probably also battling malnutrition, an accumulation of trapped trauma and emotions, many negative beliefs, and toxic emotions.

One of the foundational understandings in holistic and energy thought is that disease is the body's best way to cope with an existing situation it cannot otherwise resolve. Let me put this into perspective. We think, on average, 60,000 thoughts a day. Like an iceberg, 95% of these thoughts are subconscious and many of them are negative. These negative thoughts are comprised of toxic energy, trauma triggers, double binds, and other highly charged negative energies. The body will attempt to resolve this negative energy, but the resolution may actually be a neg-ative symptom, physically and/or emotionally. If we begin to "empty the bowl" of negative energy by resolving double binds, releasing traumas and trapped emotions, reprograming beliefs, eating healthy, detoxing, thinking positively and saying positive things, the symptoms can often disappear because we no longer need them. Every small action we take towards positive energy changes our vibration and elevates us. Disease cannot exist at higher vibrations.

Repetition makes a new belief feel more and more true. Every time we have that series of positive thoughts and feelings, neurons associated with that positivity become more active. If we are able to completely change a be-lief, thought pattern, or emotions, the neural pathways to negative thoughts and feelings will become extinct. **The brain is reprogrammable.**

When we have new joyful experiences, new neurons fire together. When the existing neurons no longer fire together, they unwire. When new positive connections are made and fire together, they continue to connect, making new systems of neural pathways. We have to be inten-tional until this becomes automatic. We have to rehearse and meditate on our new beliefs in order to reprogram our brain and feel good.

When we are in a state of heightened emotions, we are in an alpha brainwave state. Our normal waking state is beta. Theta is our subconscious state, our dream state, and the state in deep meditation or hypnosis. Delta is the lowest state when our brain is working on repairing and recharging our body. When we are in active beta, we are more guarded and less impressionable. Children's brains start out in delta until about two-years-old, then move to mostly theta from two to six-years-old, and then to alpha from seven to twelve-years-old. This is evidence that children are highly impressionable. They give meaning to every stimulus without questioning. In fact, we could call them "meaning making machines," firing and wiring constantly, their subconscious mind dominating. They don't have the same ability to challenge their reality as adults or even children older than twelve do. They are being programmed by their experiences 24/7. This is why we consider them to be metaphorical "sponges," constantly absorbing everything around them.

Most of our beliefs will be formed by age twelve and after that, mainly just reinforced. This is why teaching children to process emotions is so critical at a young age. Helping them remain calm and return to states of peace and joy sets up their brain and subconscious for a healthy future. As I shared earlier, everything is energy and therefore in motion. Scientists have determined the brain is reprogrammable; it is not rigid, but plastic. (This is called neuroplasticity.)[lix] This means that beliefs can be reprogrammed as well. When we work to reprogram old beliefs, we see the most progress when in a state of alpha or theta waves. It is more likely to sink into our subconscious and stick when we are experiencing the deepest brain waves possible.

Most people have thousands of trapped emotions with dozens of negative beliefs attached. They may be subtle, but they feel true. Our subconscious mind is powerful because it is largely responsible for dictating our life. When we release negative emotions and consciously reprogram our thoughts, our vibration changes, what we attract changes, and our life looks very different. We were wired for peace and joy. We walk in alignment with God's truths about us when we release the negative. His truths will always align with peace and joy.

CHAPTER 12
ARE YOU A SON OR A SLAVE?

Quantum physics says the universe is neutral and our lives are a creation of what we think. In a study on brain waves, it was discovered that when human attention was given to brain waves, they collapsed into particles. From this, quantum physicists drew the conclusion that everything in our physical world is a creation of our (or God's) consciousness of it.[ix] Whatever a man has thought or dreamt will eventually manifest.

Scripture tells us the creation of the world was a thought from God (His consciousness) spoken into existence. It says repeatedly in Genesis, "And God said..." in regards to the creation of everything. God's creative power was then infused into man (Adam) when He said, "Let us make man in our image, after our likeness" (Genesis 1:26). The concept of collapse and manifestation woven throughout this book is a lot to consider and accept. It may be that, like eating an elephant, you have to consume it in small bites. It takes a while for the conscious, natural mind to grasp intangible or multidimensional principles. Like the movie "The Matrix," we see what is in the material world and don't see what is going on in the invisible world. I encourage you to cross-study the concepts outlined here and eat the elephant bite by bite.

This idea is reiterated in Proverbs 23:7, "As a man thinks in his heart, so is he." The idea that we create our own reality is not only backed up by science, but also by scripture. When we consider that thinking in our heart determines our faith with what Jesus teaches in Matthew 7:7-12 (ask, seek and knock) and reflect where our faith lies, then we can conclude that in every area of our life, we choose to believe one of two options: we either believe that "the universe is for us" or that "the universe is against us." In various areas of our lives we may believe it is for us and in another area, it is against us. For example, if I am in great health, take no medications, and am physically fit for a woman my age, it may be easy to believe the universe is for me. On the other hand, if I continue to experience financial struggles that seem to contradict what I feel is my potential for success, I may consciously or subconsciously believe the universe is against me and my finances.

Scripturally, we see this same paradigm using the contrast of sons and slaves. In my experience, the church can often make us feel worthless, using the scripture that says our "righteousness is as filthy rags" (Isaiah 64:6) to make us believe we deserve nothing good in our lives. We believe we must work really hard to show God how grateful we are for our salvation and must earn His favor by doing great works and probably suffering. Some sects of the church use guilt and condemnation to keep their congregation loyal to a version of God who demands our sacrifice and devotion. I have spent countless hours counseling and ministering to people who have embraced this slave mentality and they consistently lack many of the fruits of the Spirit. They manifest psychological, emotional, and physical problems as a result of adhering to this slave paradigm. Low self-esteem, self-hatred, and resentment lie at the root of most relational, physical, and mental illness. Is this what God intended?

I don't want to avoid the obvious theological concept that runs throughout scripture comparing slavery and servitude to Christ. At first glance, we might think this is a contradiction to the concept of being a son, however, I believe they are separate concepts that align together. The best way to show this alignment is through the relationship between a king and a prince. While the prince is indeed a son of the king, he is given nearly the full authority of the king, ruling the kingdom as one with his father. In a healthy relationship, the king loves his son as much as he loves his own life and is willing to die for him. Even though the prince rules alongside the king, he is still considered the king's servant and must submit to his decisions and carry out his orders. This reflects a military position (the army of God) and relates to what we "do" without taking away from the position of son, which is who we "are." The two ideas reflect the distinction of doing vs. being. They are not mutually exclusive. Unfortunately, many Christians take on a "slave" mentality, as in unworthiness, because of "father wounds." These wounds are created in those who did not grow up experiencing God's intended paradigm of sonship which lead them to take on a yoke of slavery. Unfortunately, a deep-seated sense of "unworthiness" related to these wounds will not manifest fruit. I love the words of the song, "Who Am I" by Casting Crowns. "Not because of who I am, but because of what You've done, not because of what I've done, but because of who You are." The paradox is that we are more than worthy, but not because of anything we have or could ever do to earn it. Nonetheless, the authority of God will be manifested on the earth by *sons not by slaves* according to Romans 8:19.

We often glamorize this idea of "suffering for Jesus" as being highly spiritual. The ability to serve God as a son is much more like the character of God and the model He intended when He created the family model. I often see that the deepest and most life-altering wounds in people are those that came in relationship to their father and mother. God is both masculine and feminine, the embodiment of both mother and father. He created Adam and Eve in His likeness, so He is both male and female. The family model's purpose is to continually recreate the consciousness of the intended relationship He wants us (His children) to have with Him. Children were not created to be slaves (although many oppressed cultures believe this is what children are bred for). Perhaps the best model of how God feels about us can be seen in Luke 15:11-32 (NIV) where Jesus tells the story of the prodigal son. Parts of my understanding of sonship came from teachings on the prodigal son during the many years I attended the powerful bible study in Dallas, Texas, led by Geroge Burriss.

Just prior to the story of the prodigal son, Jesus shares the parable of the lost sheep and lost coin. In both stories, the owner of the sheep and coin leave the rest of their charge to find the one that was lost and rejoice greatly when they find it. These stories act as a segue into the parable of the prodigal son. It is important that you know "prodigal" means "characterized by profuse or wasteful expenditure or lavish or recklessly **spendthrift**."[lxi]

In the parable of the prodigal son, the youngest son of a household leaves home with his inheritance and squanders it on the equivalent of booze, women, and drugs. After all his money is spent and all of his "friends" leave, he cannot find a job, sleeps in the pigpen, and is pretty much stripped of any remaining dignity. He returns home to beg for a slave's position in his father's house, but his father's reaction is not what he expects:

> But, while he was still a long way off, his father saw him and was filled with compassion for him; he ran to his son, threw his arms around him and kissed him.
> 21The son said to him, "Father, I have sinned against heaven and against you. I am no longer worthy to be called your son."
> 22But the father said to his servants, "Quick! Bring the best **robe** and put it on him. Put a **ring** on his finger and **sandals** on his feet. 23Bring the fattened calf and kill it. Let's have a **feast and celebrate**. 24For this son of mine was dead and is alive again; he was lost and is found." So they began to celebrate. (Luke 15:20-24)

How could anyone read these three parables and not understand that Jesus is clearly telling us that God desperately loves each of his children? The robe, ring, and sandals are all tokens in this culture of being a son. Each day when we cry out to God to forgive us of our wrongdoings or thoughts, He, once again, puts a ring, robe, and sandals on us. Sons serve their father with joy and peace. Sons are provided for by their fathers. Sons are deeply and unconditionally loved. Sons walk in the love of the father. Sons vibrate high.

Many of us do not resonate with sonship because our parents did not model the Father's love, causing us deep wounds. The other reason we do not believe we are sons can be illustrated by the older brother.

> 28The older brother became angry and refused to go in. So his father went out and pleaded with him. 29But he answered his

119

father, "Look! All these years I've been slaving for you and never disobeyed your orders. Yet you never gave me even a young goat so I could celebrate with my friends. [30]But when this son of yours who has squandered your property with prostitutes comes home, you kill the fattened calf for him!"

Somehow, the religious spirit enters the church and we forget we are sons and become slaves. We lose our love relationship with God and suddenly are driven to be good and work hard for the kingdom, forgetting to cultivate our continually transformational relationship with Him. We then move back into our comfortable familiarity of the world by comparing ourselves to others. This of course leads to judgment, gossip, offense, and all the things we thought we left behind. We become the older brother after working so hard not to.

The world we live in is a "performance-based-acceptance" world. It begins as soon as we can talk and is reinforced every day, in school, work, and every arena of life. God's love is truly unconditional. He sees us as complete and whole in Christ, and we are adored simply because we are His sons. The minute we believe we have worked to earn the Father's approval, we become religious like the older son.

Remember that "prodigal" means wasteful or recklessly lavish. Doesn't that sound like the story of the sinful woman and the alabaster jar in Luke 7:36? It was expensive and extravagant; she poured it out on Him, along with her jar of tears. It was wasteful. She had no one to impress; it was out of a type of gratitude only prodigals understand.

God wasted Jesus' life for us. God too is a prodigal. Jesus was poured out. Remember he didn't just die for us. He was betrayed, humiliated, rejected, cursed, and tortured first. Have you ever been in love and had your heart broken? No intensity of anguish that love has ever caused us will match those that Jesus felt out of His love for us. Most would concur that His value was so much greater than the value of the focus of His sacrifice, but God doesn't agree. Extravagance requires passion and devotion. This implies intimacy and relationship, not performance. God anguishes over wanting relationship with us.

Finally, the father wanted to throw the son a party for returning home. The older brother was mad; the father had never offered to throw him a party. The father tells him he would have gladly held a banquet if the older son had ever asked. Jesus has a perpetual banquet and feast going on with an open invitation (Revelation 3:20). It is His desire to celebrate us and celebrate with us for all eternity. Fathers don't celebrate slaves, just sons.

Ambassadors for Christ

One of the other roles of the prince is to negotiate peace. Jesus is the "Prince of Peace." Remember we said that the word "blessing" meant "God's intention"? When we walk in our role as sons, we are ambassadors of peace. Our words and declarations carry the authority of the King and He calls us specifically to walk with the intention of blessing. We are ambassadors with men and warriors against the spirits opposed to God. We don't war with men (Ephesians 6:12). Sons are servants of peace with a deliberate mission to bring peace between men and God. This is a great commission as it calls us to lay our judgments, opinions, and offenses aside to do the job.

The New Testament letters focus on the works and power of the Holy Spirit. The Holy Spirit is the power and authority of the Father that was conferred to man at Pentecost. Jesus told us He would send a helper so that we would do greater works (John 14-15). Good kings delegate their authority to their sons and heirs, not to slaves. Authority is given to those who have the position to do what their leader delegates to them. Princes rode into battle to serve the kingdom of their father. They never doubted the position that they held. Princes do not question their wealth, but recognize their responsibility with the management of it.

This concept of authority as sons (and not slaves) is significant when we discuss the law of attraction. Princes have different expectations regarding their life as opposed to slaves. Princes focus or give energy to different things than slaves, thinking differently about their life. Slaves have limitations on their beliefs, but princes believe they will one day rule and reign over everything that belongs to the king.

Jesus refers to the church as his "bride." Believers are referred to as coheirs (brothers) and brides (princesses), both of which imply royalty and position in the kingdom as family and related to God.

In Matthew 16:19, Jesus tells Peter that on the revelation of Him (Jesus) being the Christ ("on this rock"), He will build His kingdom (the kingdom of God):

> "I will give you the keys of the Kingdom of Heaven; whatever you bind on earth will be bound in heaven, and whatever you loose on earth will be loosed in heaven."

In Roman culture, only kings were given keys. Jesus is telling Peter that we will walk in kingly authority, something slaves do not have the ability to do. Sons are kings in the making and have been given authority to bring heaven to earth based on the impartation Christ promised to give us. When we know who we are as sons, we walk differently than those trying to earn God's love and acceptance.

If your desire has been to walk in greater authority in the spirit realm, then consider this important concept of sonship. Walking in power means our words, prayers, and declarations have a greater impact. Consider your current level of stewardship with your words, thoughts, and intentions. Can God trust you with greater power? Are you stewarding your current level of power well? Are you mindful and aware of what you think, say, and intend?

I believe that having a true revelation of sonship is more complicated than a mental agreement. It requires God rooting out the deepest places of unworthiness, shame, and self-hatred and restoring those places with love. It's not about knowledge of the word, it's about knowing we are loved as children of our Abba/daddy **We must truly know we are loved in order to love others (Matthew 22:37).**

Sonship is a result of subconscious alignment in a trusting, intimate relationship with the King. It is about relationship, not power. Princes can abuse the king's authority, but those who love their father do not do so, as they would not want to dishonor him. Sons manifest the heart of love that exists between them and their father, allowing them to pour out the real fruit of love on his subjects (God's other children).

Remember, the **KINGDOM** (place of royal power) **of God** (Father/Creator) **IS** (is equal to) **righteousness** (clear conscience/right standing with God which is through grace, not performance), **peace** (absence of fear and worry; slaves worry about their performance, sons don't), **and joy** (being glad together). Joy is the unbreakable connection to the Holy Spirit. Having to perform to feel loved causes feelings of fluctuation in our relationships; unconditional love from the Holy Spirit does not fluctuate (Romans 14:17).

The next verse says, "It is in this way we have the favor of God and men." We can vibrate at the frequency of peace and joy because:

- We have no fear of God rejecting us.
- We have accepted our position as sons and the implications that come with this.
- We understand that we can never earn His love, but can still receive it unconditionally.
- We actively apply grace to our lives everyday and keep our conscience clear.
- We work at walking in alignment with scripture.
- We release subconscious beliefs and replace them with hope and truth.

Using some of the practices suggested in this book, we can raise our vibration higher towards peace and joy. As this occurs, we will find that life shows us more favor and we will begin to expect more favor subconsciously. We begin to attract what we believe. Most people unknowingly believe that the universe (not God) is either for or against us. This subconscious belief is primarily created based on what we have been taught and experienced.

For years, I knew God loved me deeply and unconditionally, but I still believed "life" somehow was thwarting me from thriving in certain areas. I understood that God was continually transforming me, but lived in frustration as it seemed I wasn't receiving the abundance of His blessings my peers were. After I learned about these principles of programming, I began to separate the beliefs I had about money, ministry, and men from my relationship with the Lord. Everyday as I would wake up, I practiced meditation in efforts to reprogram my beliefs during my highest state of alpha brain waves. One morning, as I was particularly focusing on the three areas mentioned above, I heard the distinct voice of the Holy Spirit say, "You can't screw this up." I knew he was referring to my future in these three areas. I had a major revelation in that moment about how much of the day I was subconsciously worrying about making decisions for fear of "screwing up" my future. I found several instances in my adult life where decisions I made had really disastrous outcomes. In that moment, I realized that although I knew the Lord loved me unconditionally, I still believed I had to do everything right in order to have abundance. In these areas, I was still completely immersed in a performance-based mindset. I believed if I made even a minor mistake in my finances, I wouldn't prosper. If I went on a date and didn't say all the right things, it wouldn't work out. If I misspoke in a counseling session, then my ministry would be sabotaged. I believed if I made a mistake, bad things would happen, manifesting the belief that the universe was against me.

While God was revealing these issues to me, I had a revelation that if I continued to let my vibration remain in a state of fear and worry (very low vibrations), I would attract the opposite of favor (like attracts like). It was absolutely necessary that I shift my mindset to one of peace and joy in order to receive favor from God. Matthew 6:33 (NASB) says:

"But seek first His kingdom and His righteousness, and ALL these things will be added to you."

A few verses before this in Matthew 6:26 (NIV) it says:

"Look at the birds of the air; they do not sow or reap or store away in barns, and yet your Heavenly Father feeds them. Are you not much more valuable than they?"

Even though I believed I had been healed of performance-based acceptance/perfectionism earlier in life, I had the clear revelation that I still believed the universe required perfection from me. When we believe we have to work for everything we get (money, love, success, etc.), then God does not need to show us favor. Believing I am the son of a king in my heart also means I believe that I don't have to strive for or worry about recieving His abundance. Do little children in a loving family worry about working hard for their father's love? They know they are not capable of earning a living to support their family. Spiritually, we are toddlers in the hand of an almighty God. It is silly to think we can do anything great in and of ourselves.

I recognized I was in a double bind and had made a habit of second-guessing every decision out of fear. Believing a loving Father wanted me to walk in abundance that required no performance, just a deep change in belief, was a difficult shift in mindset. I began to release all the trapped emotions and events that were tied to this negative belief system. I knew in order to "walk the talk" I was teaching, I had to walk in peace knowing I couldn't "screw it up." I realized I made choices based on what I "should" do rather than what I wanted. Getting what I wanted was not usually a thought at all. My heart's desires were a seemingly hopeless pipe dream.

Since these revelations, my life has changed significantly. I make choices based on what I want (and as my wants are aligned with God's wants, then this manifests easily). I believe I attract God's favor (and man's favor) and my decisions always seem to work out. My life is evidence of the outcome of raising my vibration. The fruit of every area of my life reflects that of a higher vibration being. Because I have closed that door to generational curses in my life and raised my personal vibration, I seem to receive minimal negative backlash from the spiritual world, which constantly amazes me. I forgive, repent daily, and walk in gratitude. I practice (not perfectly) most of the principles I have discussed in this book daily. Life has a flow and I am still making new shifts every day. It's a lifetime process.

Living as a son and walking in the promises of the kingdom of God is a very different experience of life than most people realize. We don't know what we don't know until those quiet little messages creep up from our subconscious to tell us the "truth" of what we actually believe. While I am committed to continually raising my vibration in every arena of my life, I already experience an unprecedented amount of peace and freedom daily. I see more fruit in my life than ever before. I strongly encourage you to meditate on the principles I share in this book. Testimonies consistently come forth that prove they are powerful and they work. Anyone can do it by making small shifts. It's just one small bite at time — progress, not perfection.

CHAPTER 13
CHANGING YOUR VIBRATION

There are four stages of learning/transformation. The first stage is being "subconsciously incompetent." This is the stage of "I don't know what I don't know." People in this stage believe they are a helpless participant in a universe that is against them and find themselves reacting in uncontrollable rage when its unnecessary and unprecedented. The second stage of transformation is "conscious incompetence." In this stage, people realize they are responsible for their negative reactions, emotions, and beliefs, but don't know how to fix them. They realize their anger, but can't identify the trigger or control the reaction. The third stage is "conscious competence." In this stage, people will still feel anger, but can recognize their triggers and pivot or manage the feeling without raging and damaging others. I still feel the triggered response but have more self-control and know it is my issue and don't blame the other person. The fourth stage is "subconscious competence." People are successfully in this stage when they have identified and released their triggers and have no emotional reaction to their anger. The subconscious has effectively shifted and there is noticeable fruit manifested.

When we start something new, we have to work until we become consciously competent at it and, eventually, we do it automatically, meaning we have mastered subconscious competence. I desperately want God to trust me with His authority. I desperately want people to be healed in my presence. I desperately want to see the kingdom of God manifested on earth. If you resonate with these statements as well, then work to become "subconsciously competent" at the following practical steps so you can live a transformed life. The steps must be followed deliberately and some require more energy than others, but the fruit is worth the effort.

I like to use the metaphor of being a hot air balloon as part of my education process. Hot air balloons have two components that affect the altitude (frequency) of the balloon (think of the balloon as you and I). What makes the balloon soar high is hydrogen (hot air) and what keeps the balloon grounded are sandbags. When we remove all sandbags and have sufficient hot air, we can take the balloon as high as we choose. From a vibrational perspective, when we identify things that have lowered our frequency, we need to remove them (like the sandbags) in order to rise. We also need to find things to raise us up (like the hot air) in order to raise our frequency. It's like simple math: subtract the bad and add the good.

Things that Lower Frequency

Anything that makes you feel down lowers your frequency. The following are some examples of things I have found to lower frequency:

- **Control and Resistance**: Control and/or the manipulation of others and our situations is motivated out of fear and worry. Fear of being controlled by others, even God, also lowers frequency. Fear is low vibration and will never produce good fruit.
- **Judgments, Curses, and Resentment**: As we discussed in chapter five, these are low vibration thoughts and words that attract negative things. Feelings of fear, anxiety, depression, anger, guilt, shame, jealousy, and envy all have a low frequency. When they are trapped, they contribute to belief systems which are negative. ("The universe is against me.") Whether we are committing these in thought or deed, against ourselves or others, all will lower our frequency.
- **Alcohol, Smoking, and Prescription and Recreational Drugs**: Although these may make you feel better temporarily, they lower frequency and are not legitimate ways to reduce stress.

- **Food**: Fresh, live food has a high frequency. Processed foods have a low frequency and, therefore, lower the frequency of your body. Pesticides and toxins also lower frequency.
- **Lack of Exercise, Sleep, and Water**: Not taking care of our physical needs lowers frequency.
- **Negative Environment**: Other people's frequencies can raise or lower our own depending on the situation. Gossip, judging, pessimism, and fearmongering lower our vibration and frequency
- **Pornography and Horror**: Inappropriate sexual stimuli bring arousal and eventually connect to shame. When what we view is degrading, dark, evil, terrifying, or satanic, we lower our vibration. These things are also portals that give the enemy of our soul legal access to afflict us.
- **Environmental Toxins**: Toxins we absorb from food, water, chemtrails, EMFs/dirty electricity (electronics), pesticides, chemicals in construction materials, and products of commercial industry and agriculture have the ability to lower our vibration.
- **Toxins We Unknowingly Do to Ourselves**: Vaccines, plastics, candles, chemicals from cleaning products, perfumes, antiperspirant, lotions and cosmetics, and hair dye can effectively lower our vibration depending on their ingredients. Our skin is the largest porous organ in our body designed to detox and we continually toxify our body with what we put on our skin. This lowers our vibration.
- **Music and Sound**: Our ears respond to vibrations. Remember the results of Dr. Masaru Emoto's tests: heavy metal music left chaotic, dissonant patterns in the water and classical music made pretty snowflakes.[lxii]

Steps to Change Our Subconscious Beliefs

People who have dissociated to cope with trauma have symptoms of Dissociative Identity Disorder or DID. This is a recognized diagnosis in the Professional Psychological Community and is found on the DSM 5

(Diagnostic and Statistical Manual). DID was formerly known as Multiple Personality Disorder or MPD. Because people can have what are known as fractures, parts or "alters" which may not show up as full-blown amnesiac or different personalities, the American Psychological Association changed the diagnosis to DID to cover a broader spectrum of symptoms. If you study cults and developed methods of brainwashing, you will find there are well-developed procedures for programming the mind. Satanic ritual abuse involves repeated trauma starting at a young age. A child's brain dissociates under certain amounts of real trauma and even under perceived threats. In this state of dissociating, new information can be programmed into the mind. Cults cause dissociation in children, forming multiple personalities, parts, or alters, and give these parts secret information useful to the cult, but dangerous for anyone else to know. These parts are conditioned to manifest under certain triggers when the stored information is important.

Dissociation is not used exclusively by cults. Militaries across the globe have been know to brainwash their members and those they capture. There are documented sources of the U.S military's use of MKUltra and Monarch Programming. Novels and movies like *The Bourne Trilogy* and *Manchurian Candidate* prompt us to consider the accessibility of the subconscious. If this technique can be used in these various venues, why can't we use it to change our subconscious beliefs?

Once belief systems are created and reinforced, they may become very stable, even if irrational. If emotions are intense enough, the abuse victim's brain will completely disconnect from the occurrence of the event (using repression or amnesia), but leave behind the belief system. The hippocampus is the brain part responsible for chronological or explicit memory. The amygdala is the brain part that is looking out for danger. If the amygdala decides something is dangerous enough, the memory is not allowed into the hippocampus. Many traumatic events are not easily accessed by conscious memory, but definitely stored in the subconscious.[lxiii]

Like heart memory, quantum physics studies have proven that everything we experience is recorded somewhere within our being, even if the conscious mind does not remember.[lxiv] This explains why memories can occur even when the brain is not accessing them. When this belief or memory is triggered, the body reacts as if it is happening in that moment, a phenomenon called an abreaction. Soldiers manifesting PTSD can legitimately feel like someone is watching them at all times or that they are in danger. Their hypervigilance is a manifestation of a deep subconscious belief system programmed when they were truly unsafe and in a heightened state of emotion. All of us have this to some degree, although possibly not in such an extreme fashion.

I once had a client who was seeking therapy in preparation for making a speech at his daughter's wedding. Every time he spoke in front of a crowd, he would break out into a sweat that would drench his clothes. Clearly, this was not a normal reaction, even taking into account typical nerves. After a few sessions, we uncovered that he had a lot of trauma in his childhood, much of which he did not remember. We worked on releasing a great deal of feelings related to humiliation and helplessness while reprogramming his beliefs about his identity. We also managed some symptoms of anxiety through oils and supplements. When it came time for his daughter's wedding, he pulled off the speech without a drop of sweat. His fear of being humiliated and powerless was stored in his subconscious mind.

Another one of my clients had experienced abandonment in her prememory years. Whenever her husband would go out of town or not be home in the evening, she would have panic attacks for no particular reason. Both of these clients' amygdalas had prevented traumatic memories from being stored in the hippocampus, but the energy was still buried in their subconscious (or heart) and was triggered when they experienced similar situations to those traumatic events. Many of our subconscious beliefs are not connected specifically to our current situations, but are still triggered by cues that cause similar emotions.

We can use this knowledge to deliberately reprogram our subconscious from negative to positive. Below, I have outlined three steps to transformation — the reprogramming process I use with clients to help them begin to attract positive vibrations and eventually bring them to a state of greater peace and joy. My prayer is that you will apply these steps into your life so you can thrive.

Three Steps to Transformation

The first step towards transformation is to release trapped emotions, vows, and judgments. Chapter eleven contained a comprehensive explanation of what connects the "wires" or neurons in our brain and how emotions can become trapped. After years of working in the field of inner healing, I have come to understand the following process: our painful experiences create judgments, vows, and deep-rooted belief systems about ourselves, others, life, God, and "the universe." As I just stated, this occurs when there is heightened emotion, particularly negative. The situation does not have to necessarily be traumatic, just heightened. Prayer ministry and muscle testing help uncover the deeply rooted judgments and beliefs that control our subconscious belief systems. Our emotions follow our beliefs, which affect our behavior, which affects our vibration and thus, affecting our attraction.

As I explained in the chapter on bitter roots judgement, we attract from the judgments we make. The problem is in finding those judgments. When they are deeply rooted, we don't even know we believe them. After years of being involved in ministry, I still felt there were pieces missing as I observed how people lived their lives after receiving ministry. I saw many people receive immediate relief, but after some time passed, they went back to many of the same old belief systems. One of these pieces of the puzzle manifested to me when I learned about trapped emotions. I had personally spent many years releasing judgments against my family members, but I still noticed I had pain attached to many memories involving them. I also noticed that all the good decisions I had made to replace the judgments had not completely bloomed, although I did see some good fruit in my life.

When I started releasing the trapped emotions, I found a new level of peace. This release was necessary for me to take captive thoughts of worry and experience true peace and joy. As a highly empathetic person,

I feel my emotions and those of other people intensely. I realized I had spent the first twenty-one years of my life stuffing these emotions away, never fully processing them. This step towards release created an opportunity for me to reprogram my heart/subconscious with new beliefs.

I had tried some reprogramming techniques already, but discovered they wouldn't take root until I released the trapped emotions. Now, when I am laying out my requests before the Lord (using attraction/prayer techniques), I test myself to see if there are any trapped emotions that would keep me from truly believing my request(s) will come to pass. The answer always seems to be "yes." I find there are always judgments that prevent me from believing I can have the things I desire. Often, the memories attached to these judgements are not highly traumatic, but have caused me to draw my own conclusions about myself, life (or the universe), God, and so on. Almost every day, God reveals some new area in my life that is driven by subtle beliefs that don't align with His truth. The release process is a lifelong journey of transformation.

Step two is to make space for new subconscious belief systems. Even though I had recognized the subconscious judgments and vows, and had repented for them, I still could not access complete transformation. I failed to realize that once I released the trapped emotions, vows, curses, and judgments, I had to fill that space with a new belief system. This is reprogramming. If we don't do this, the void will be filled with what is familiar and comfortable. In terms of the law of attraction, right after releasing the old, we must start visualizing and attracting the new. The time delay between the release of the old vibration and the arrival of the new vibration may allow for those familiar, negative things to return. This means our reprogramming needs to be deliberate. According to my personal work, it takes (on average) a few months of trapped emotions sessions for there to be a pattern of new fruit manifested.

This was another piece missing from some of the inner healing models I had previously learned and implemented. New beliefs were stated, but the practice of and science behind rooting them deeply was not taught. Christians are often told by Christian counselors the answer to solving their deeply rooted problems is to read more scripture and pray more. While these are all great practices to implement, the subconscious is more powerful than the conscious mind and thus the conscious mind cannot change the subconscious through left-brained repetition exercises.

Most of the people who end up in a therapist's office claim that this process based on repitition didn't work. The truth is not that scripture or praying wasn't helpful, but that the distress in their hearts/subconscious prevented them from changing their deeply rooted thoughts. The trapped emotions and beliefs were not accessible by the left brain (used in memorizing). While declarations are powerful, if the subconscious is resolute in its belief systems, the left brain loses the battle. Deliberate follow-up is the key.

The last step is to find techniques that deliberately reprogram the subconscious with Godly beliefs. One of the best ways to reprogram is to visualize the desired changes in both the conscious and subconscious belief systems. When we visualize and create vivid images in our conscious mind, we produce a positive heightened emotion (instead of negative). This gives us access to the void left over from the removal of the old beliefs and waters that new belief seed.

For example, if you didn't feel loved by your mother as a child, but you release the pain, bitterness, and judgment regarding this and visualize yourself (as a child) feeling loved by your mom, in effect, you can rewrite history, creating a new belief deep within your heart that states your mom loved you. This may seem odd, but remember that when you visualize, your brain can't distinguish between reality and imagination. By fully engaging our imagination, we fool the brain into believing this new belief is a true experience and rewrite a new truth on the subconscious. Another effective approach used by those in inner healing is to invite the Holy Spirit into that memory and see if He will speak a truth deep into our soul. This works best with those who have very strong relationships with the Lord already as it could possibly bring shame to those who may not see or hear from God. God's presence has the power to produce a vision of Him being present with His love. This is a powerful way to change a negative belief through the love of an omnipresent source.

Like I mentioned previously, the process I use in my personal practice (and recommend you use) allows clients to release old trapped emotions and beliefs and replace them with new desired beliefs and emotions. There are certainly other techniques that may provide the same results, but the technique mentioned is one that has worked for me personally and professionally. Still, using daily techniques to reinforce these new, Godly belief systems is key to sealing the change in the subconscious.

It helps to create structures for consistency. I can give a client vitamins to help change their health, but they have to remember to take them everyday. The same is true with reprogramming homework. Some people are excited to practice and others need some help or accountability. Journals, apps, programs, or simply creating a daily routine that incorporates reprogramming are great ways to implement this sort of accountability. (There are many free, online resources available to help you reach your goals.) The old beliefs were reinforced with repetition, so the new beliefs need to be repeated consciously in order to take root as well.

I want to share a very personal story of how quickly I was reprogrammed by a new thought. Over the years, I have spent many hours healing and uprooting judgments from my own heart. Objectively speaking, my childhood was not very traumatic, but I am a highly sensitive person so many of my experiences created trapped emotions. I have spent countless hours recovering from the hurt I felt from my mother. I came to a place where I felt I had truly forgiven her, made space for new, positive beliefs about her, and repented of my judgments towards her. My mom died of cancer in 1997, but between diagnosis and death, we had some wonderful times of restoration. Still, in my subconscious, there remained the belief that she never really loved me as a child.

One day, I was reviewing *The Five Love Languages* by Gary Chapman.[lxv] My love languages are "physical touch" and "words of affirmation." (The other three languages are "gifts," "quality time," and "acts of service.") As I read, I was meditating on my own children's love languages and realized that I was not deliberate in speaking to them in their languages. I had a sudden revelation that my mom's love languages were quality time and gifts. At this very moment, deep in my spirit, my heart went from not feeling loved by her to knowing I was loved. In a flash, I relived all the time she spent playing games with me, reviewing classic books, teaching me ballroom dancing, taking me shopping, etc. My whole childhood was relived in a moment. I eventually made space in my heart for new, positive beliefs about her, but in this moment, I relived my childhood from a consciousness of being loved.

Another way to reprogram the subconscious is demonstrated in the book *The Healing Code* by Alex Loyd.[lxvi] I began to practice healing codes prior to discovering the trapped emotion paradigm in an attempt to energize and relieve stress. Healing codes are energy points around the face that create an energy circuit. Loyd believes when positive affirmations are spoken while moving the hands (creating an energy circuit), the subconscious is successfully reprogrammed. The process includes visualization as well. The theory is that by doing this while connected to the body's energy system, the intentions and images travel deeper into and are more effective in changing the subconscious. While I found this process helpful, I did not see the same results as when I identified and released the trapped emotions that caused the negative beliefs in the first place.

When we use techniques that involve all three of the elements detailed above, we engage our body, soul, and spirit to the things we desire. Words are the language of the soul, images are the language of the spirit, and sounds are the language of the body. Declare God's promises continually as part of what you visualize. Remember the repeated premise of this book includes the power of thought, emotion, and words to bring transformation. Declarations are powerful. The same power that created the universe (the Holy Spirit) dwells in you. Whether or not you believe in the power of the prophetic, I have never met a Christian who does not believe that God has promised them something specific. How God communicated that to them may vary from person to person, but everyone believes God has put something strongly in their spirit. Most people can quote Psalms 37:4 (AMP):

Delight yourself also in the Lord and He will give you the desires and secret petitions of your heart.

We all have secret desires we are hoping for God to fulfill as we seek Him. Remember that feeling what you want and visualizing is key to changing your subconscious beliefs, vibrations, and attraction. Our heart may speak its desires to God, but often those desires contradict our programmed beliefs. Sons believe loving fathers will give them their desires, as long as those desires are for the best. When we review our beliefs and challenge them (often this requires another person or counselor), we often see that our core beliefs about what we deserve do not line up with our desires. Our "faith" or theology may be overriding what we want.

Various techniques you can use to access your subconscious beliefs are quoting scriptural promises made to all believers, scriptures and revelations you have received in your quiet time, and even some of the specific, personal promises God has given to you. Using these techniques ensures the core reprogramming aligns with and is obedient to God's will while broadening your faith.

Changing Conscious Beliefs, Words, Thoughts, and Vibrations

I want to challenge you by asking: how teachable are you? Many of us believe we are teachable, but refuse to change in the areas that matter most. Change occurs when we deliberately decide we are willing to do *whatever it takes* to transform. (Addiction recovery is an example of this "whatever it takes" principle. You must be all in for it to be effective.) Change is not rapid. We are not wired for rapid transformation and our brain cannot manage it. When we are deliberate, intentional, and consistent with these gradual changes, it makes an impact on our vibration and helps us to reach our goals. Take a few minutes and consider your willingness to change before you choose to do "whatever it takes."

I have discussed 2 Corinthians 10:5 (taking thoughts captive), Philippians 4:6-8 (do not be anxious), James 3:9-10 (praise and curse with the same tongue), and other scriptures we all know, but don't seem to practice. The real issue is that we are not paying attention to what we think and we allow our subconscious to rule our lives. Becoming aware of what we think takes practice. After we have brought awareness to our thinking, challenging it will also take practice.

When you read the chapter on bitter root judgments, did you find that you were not aware of your constant judgement towards other people? Changing conscious beliefs starts with being self-aware. Another motivation to changing beliefs is accepting the paradigm laid out in this book as truth. If you don't truly believe that everything you think, believe, and say dictates the course of your life, then you won't make an effort to change it. We all put energy into things that matter to us and motivate us. If you are truly motivated to change your life, then you will put energy into changing your vibration. Here are some ways you can do this:

1. **Take worry captive**. Worry is a form of fear and control and it vibrates low. I was raised to believe that "responsible people worry." My whole life I believed this was true. I knew that according to Matthew 6, worrying was not trusting God, but I didn't know how to stop worrying. After understanding the truth in Romans 14:17, I found that worry was producing results contrary to what I wanted to achieve and not at all reflecting the kingdom of God. Once I understood that the most effective place I could be was in a state of peace, joy, love, and gratitude, I had the motivation I needed to take worry captive with vigor.

2. **Practice gratitude**. All of the fruits of the spirit measure on a high-frequency wavelength. Disciplining ourselves to practice gratitude helps us shift our thoughts when we are stuck in the negative. The Bible tells us to "put on a garment of praise for a spirit of heaviness" (Isaiah 61:3). When we think negatively, we send out a low attraction to attract more negative. The law of attraction doesn't know the word "don't." Whatever you think about is what you attract, therefore, think about what you want, not what you don't want.

3. **Smile for a minute or two**. You cannot think negatively when you are truly smiling. Include things in your life that make you laugh and smile frequently.

4. **Avoid negative news and allow other people to have a different perception or opinion than you.** I don't watch the news at all, nor do I engage in political discussions or arguments. Everyone is entitled to an opinion and a perception. In many arenas, there is not a right or wrong, there are only viewpoints and opinions. Different perceptions keep us open to evaluating what we truly believe, adhere to, and trust. (Remember the definitions of belief and faith.) While the tenets of Christianity are generally agreed upon through most denominations, many other areas are cause for dissension, disagreement, and judgment. I once read a quote by Rick Joyner that said, "In the main tenets (of Christianity), there should be unity, in the fringe areas, liberty, and in ALL things, charity (love)." We should love everyone whether or not they agree with our doctrine. Take each part of Philippians 4:8 and replace the word "whatever" with your name. Practice these things. Think of something good, then think of something lovely, and so on. These are the practices that change your thinking.

5. **Avoid negative people. Choose people (or pets) who celebrate you**. This is not entirely possible all the time, but within the realm you have power over, surround yourself with affirming, encouraging people who see the glass half-full (or overflowing). I have certain opinions about things, but I rarely engage in arguments. I don't believe there has to be a wrong and right. Debate is a power struggle to make someone wrong and create low vibrations in the atmosphere. It's okay to stand up for what you believe in, but pay attention to whether your words are manifesting the fruit of the spirit. We are more powerful when we enable other people to also be powerful. Remember the definition of God's will in Ephesians 5:17-20:

    > [1]Therefore do not be vague and thoughtless and foolish, but understanding and firmly grasping what the will of the Lord is. [18]And do not get drunk with wine, for that is debauchery; but ever be filled and

stimulated with the [Holy] Spirit. [19]Speak out to one another in psalms and hymns and spiritual songs, offering praise with voices and instru ments] and making melody with all your heart to the Lord, [20]at all times and for everything giving thanks in the name of our Lord Jesus Christ to God the Father.

Love creates a higher frequency in both the giving and re- ceiving of it. Being around people who seem to uncondi- tionally care for us, like our pets, creates an elevated mood and thus and elevated frequency. When we love others, they can entrain to a higher vibration and vice versa. When we are surrounded by this type of energy on a regular basis, we have greater success in staying at a higher frequency and loving others.

6. **Forgive quickly when someone hurts you. Choose to bless them and repent of judging them.** Pay attention to the thought "I would never do that." Pay attention to thoughts of superiority or inferiority. These are low vibration thoughts. When you catch yourself thinking in this way, take those thoughts captive. One of the things I love most about my friends is they say amazing things to encourage me (words of affirmation is one of my love languages) and often it disarms me because I realize that my subconscious beliefs don't align with how they see me. Being around people who love you is a great way to change your beliefs about yourself and raise your vibration.

7. **Memorize or have access to scripture.** When we catch our- selves thinking something that contradicts what God says about us, we should practice immediately accessing scripture in order to challenge that belief. Taking time to memorize scripture is helpful in taking thoughts captive. Buy a book of God's promises and keep daily devotionals readily available. I have a list of God's promises He has made to me personally that I remind Him and

myself of each day. We don't actually have to remind God, He has not forgotten, but like Jacob, there is the issue of contending for His blessings (Genesis 32). Reminding Him that He has promised to bless us is creating, declaring, and contending for our promise.

8. **Begin to develop the disciplines of meditation or contemplative prayer.** Meditation and/or contemplative prayer help us to become more aware of what we are thinking. Take whatever steps necessary to learn to quiet your mind. Choose another person who has mastered this art to mentor you. Go to meditation or contemplative prayer groups and soaking prayer services. Practice tuning yourself into the Holy Spirit each day and choosing to think very deliberate thoughts. Learn how to sit, quiet yourself, and listen to Him. I will admit that I am one of those people who has a million thoughts every day. The times I have found that I listen best is when I first wake up and when I am driving. During these times, my mind is less active and I am more peaceful. Take time to choose what to think.

9. **Learn visualization techniques.** This involves a deliberate use of our imagination. Imagine what you want your life to look like. Speak what you visualize, feel it, and see yourself doing it. Use all five senses and as much detail as you can conjure up. This practice builds faith for a positive future. Remember that the brain cannot distinguish between visualizing in detail and experience; it registers the same. When our brain experiences something as real, then our faith for that thing is built. Ministers will often visualize how they want the service to go and it encourages belief for miracles and for God to move mightily. Take time to choose what you think. Earl Nightingale made a recording in 1956 after reading Napoleon Hill's book, *Think and Grow Rich.* Having the revelation, "We become what we think," he combined Hill's book with the two scriptures "As a man thinks..." and "You reap what you sow" to create techniques similar to those mentioned in *The Secret.* Nightingale became wealthy from this recording and

from exposing how all the "secret societies" know and practice this "secret" principle.[lxvii] The practice of the law of attraction has been used for decades, even from a scriptural standpoint, but has not been widely understood or popular until more recently. The body of Christ has had access to the most profound secrets of living for thousands of years, but the secular world seems to better apply these to their lives than we do as Christians. Why is this? These principles aren't hard to implement, they just take belief (faith) and practice. CHOOSE WHAT YOU THINK AND THINK WHAT YOU CHOOSE.

10. **Take time to make very deliberate affirmations of self.** I have found a meditation called "The Moses Code" that uses "I am" statements as God does in Exodus. "I am that I am" is the name of God (Exodus 3:14). While we are not saying we are God, we are made in His image and likeness (Genesis 1:27). We use "I am" statements because there is the power of the Holy Spirit dwelling in us and that power enables us to create and change. When Jesus said, "I am," in the Garden of Gethsemane (John 18:5), the power of His words caused the army to fall back. Agreeing with what God says about us in our "I am" statements, (i.e. "I am abundant, I am highly favored, I am peace, I am joy, I am loved, I am successful," etc.) aligns with the scriptures we have discussed in this book. Practice speaking the desires of your heart and the promises of God. Any area of your faith that seems to be faltering should become a focus of your "I am" statements. When I practice these statements, I can feel myself returning to a state of faith, trust, and joy from a state of distress or heightened negative emotion.

11. **Spend time with the Lord in worship.** We should want to spend time soaking in God's presence and feeling His tangible love for us. However you experience feeling connected to God (music, journaling, reading, praying, listening to teaching, etc.), then make time to do it. This is a non-doing, non-performing time. This is a receiving affirmation time.

12. **Avoid situations that create "ought to, need to, or should" obligations.** Changing beliefs means relieving oneself of the "have to" performance mentality. Remember our intention is EVERYTHING. The motive of everything we do is what creates the attraction.

13. **Choose your commitments.** If you make a commitment, you need to fulfill it. Commitments are not obligations, but choices you make.

14. **Take care of your brain.** As I already stated, we are body, soul, and spirit. Perhaps the most overlooked, ignored, and minimized part of our thinking is the physiological. Our brain is a complex organ that requires good nutrition to function. Many of us can find addiction in our ancestry. This points to a generational inheritance of low serotonin and imbalances in other brain neurochemicals. The stresses of life, diet, poor nutrition, lack of exercise, and toxic environments can add to this problem. Trapped emotions directly affect our serotonin and dopamine balances. Our brain desires homeostasis. It will use whatever memories or thoughts that have worked in the past to feel "normal." Addicts crave whatever drug makes them feel "normal." Even the most seemingly sane and happy people who smoke will tell you how nearly impossible it is to calm anxiety without a cigarette. Believers especially tend to ignore this. No one talks about the epidemic of depression, anxiety, ADHD, and other life-altering disorders we are facing in the church alone, much less in our world. Your brain chemistry directly affects your vibration. People who suffer from depression are hard-pressed to think happy thoughts and be grateful. People who struggle with anxiety can't return to peace and joy. People with OCD cannot master their thought life. The church as a whole, as well as the general population, must embrace this third part of our being. Learning to be attuned to your brain chemistry and educating yourself about what nutritional supplements are beneficial to brain power are critical to being successful. Even masters of the law of attraction

rarely talk about this. Consult a natural doctor, take the right supplements, exercise, eliminate white sugar, rest, relax, have fun, and generally take care of yourself. Make managing your own brain chemistry a priority.

15. **Decide to always pause and check your heart before you speak.** This is quite a discipline. Remember, if we really believe our words have power and authority (as sons), then choosing not to respond out of emotion, but to pause and wait is a powerful tool allowing us to maintain integrity and a high vibration. We have all been damaged by people's words and surely don't want to damage someone else out of our own hurt and anger. Remember that intention and motive determine fruit. Do we want everything burned as wood, hay, and stubble because we were hasty to respond out of our emotions (1 Corinthians 3:12-13)? I am continually learning that I must return to joy before I engage in a conversation with someone, even if that means a delay in resolving conflict. Because of my profession and my desire to stay at joy and peace, I have made the personal commitment to "react" in this manner, but I believe this is a good habit for all of us to put into practice.

16. **Examine the meaning you have given to a situation.** If you accept the paradigm that there is no objective truth in life, only our perceptions and the meaning we give them, then you can choose to examine your perceptions before reacting to a triggering experience. You decide what you feel. It is your responsibility to question your subconscious. In every situation, there is "what happened" (i.e. John stepped on my toe) and the meaning given to it (i.e. John is mad at me). The meaning given to a situation determines whether or not offense is taken. This is perception. Question whether your response is empowering or damaging to the other person. In our moments of joy and peace, we should believe we do not want to hurt anyone else, we want to empower them, but we lose this motive when our own hurts are triggered. Taking time out of a heightened state

of emotion will prevent us from damaging ourselves and others. Seeking ways to return from distress to joy and peace must be our priority. As sons of God, our goal is to be "unoffendable." Wait to speak until you know your intention is leaning towards love, hope, or peace. While we will always be confined to a body and battle fleshly desires, working towards releasing trauma, trapped emotions, and judgments from our past moves us toward a position of love.

17. **Determine to stay humble and teachable.** If we listen to others with the intent to learn rather than teach, argue, or be right, then we are always positioned in a teachable place and are less likely to move into a state of control. Remember that God resists the proud, but gives grace to the humble (James 4:6).

18. **Educate yourself on using essential oils.** In the expanding world of understanding vibration, the use of essential oils in healing continues to gain momentum. As I shared earlier, there are great benefits to essential oils and they can definitely aid in raising your vibration.

19. **Eat good organic food and drink enough water.** Every living thing has a vibration. If we put high vibration food into our bodies, we raise our frequency. Our bodies cry out for water every day (not soda, juice, etc. which are processed and have a lower frequency). Foods with chemicals, white sugar, and those that are highly processed have a low vibration. I don't advocate for any particular diet, but in general, practice eating foods as close to their original state as possible (i.e. raw fruits and vegetables).

20. **Balance adequate sleep, exercise, fun, and rest.** We must take care of our Holy Spirit temples to function well (1 Corinthians 6:19). Remember our goal is the kingdom of God. Exercise outside to get sun (vitamin D) and fresh air. Activities that bring you joy decrease stress levels and depression. Creative ventures (music, art, dance, etc.) use part of the prefrontal cortex that promotes well-being, pleasure, and joy.

21. **Supplements, EMF protectors, cleanses, chiropractic and massage therapy, and more are great ways to keep your body healthy. Toxins out, good life-giving supplements in.** We must put in positive, high-vibration elements and eliminate toxic, low vibration elements. Supplements help keep the body in healthy vibration. Electromagnetic frequency absorbers block the damaging waves we get from computers, microwaves, cell phones, and other electronics. Cleanses and colonics help the body dump low vibration toxins. Subluxations and trapped energy flow bring down negative vibrations. Wellness and caring for every system in our body keeps us at maximum physical potential.

As we take on the discipline of changing our conscious beliefs, it will segue into changing our subconscious beliefs as well. Think of your brain as a map of neuronal pathways or "roads." These pathways fire rapidly and automatically. Our way of thinking becomes akin to a certain route like we drive a certain route to work every day. Many times, we tend to be on "autopilot" and can almost make this trip with our eyes closed because it is so habitual. The same thing occurs in the pathways of our brain. They are actually burned like grooves or ruts.

If we were traveling to work one day and the road was closed due to construction, we would then have to take a detour, which would require us to pay attention and think. It takes very deliberate effort to change these ruts in our brain, but when we do it successfully and consistently, a new pathway gets burned. The more we practice our new routes or pathways, they then become ruts, but positive ruts. (Imagine if we deliberately practiced Philippians 4:8.)

CHAPTER 14
INTENTION EXPERIMENTS, PRAYER, AND SPACE/TIME

I n the experiments conducted by Dr. Emoto, we saw the effects of intention on water. Since that time, many more experiments have demonstrated the effects of the power of intention. Researcher, journalist, and author Lynn McTaggart recently set out to find objective ways to look at quantum physics, energy, and the power of concentrated thought. In her book, *The Intention Experiment* she coordinates with a number of scientists who completed studies related to intention. Her text is full of detailed experiments that scientifically prove the power of focused intention and its ability to change outcomes. Her results are not related to Christianity or any other religion, but on focused intention. The experiments also measure the physical effects that vibration, frequency, and geomagnetic stress have on consciousness. These tests confirm that intention is frequency and frequency affects external objects and people.[lxviii]

Several of the experiments detailed involved a variety of healers and "prayer masters." These authorities were not specifically Christians, but holy people representing various religions who had mastered focused intention. Prayer is the "Christian version" of focused intention. People of all religions focus their intention in some way. According to quantum physics, when intention is full of faith, belief, and joy (high frequency), it has more effective outcomes.

One of the experiments was concerning heart patients in a hospital. In a nutshell, patients were randomly selected to be prayed for by various experts in focused intention. The people praying only knew the patient's first name and were instructed to pray/send intention for healing related to heart issues. The people never met in person; they were always at a distance. The principle of non-locality in quantum physics is not limited to space. We can send prayer/intention to someone in Australia and have equal results as someone in our hometown. The results were clinically significant: the clients who received prayer/focused intention experienced better outcomes compared to those in the control group. (In an experiment, the control group receives the standard treatment or no treatment at all.) The highly experienced healers, meditators, and prayer warriors seemed to be key in the recovery of those in the experimental group. It wasn't just about intention, but about intention from those who would be considered authorities in their ability to focus thought and emotion. These experts in intention utilized the specificity of each patient's circumstance and set a strong level of compassion in their focused intentions. The results proved that the combination of these elements was statistically significant compared to each of the elements used by themselves.[lxix]

Experiments were also conducted related to using focused imagination. Muhammed Ali was famous for visualizing his fights and seeing himself win. Highly successful athletes are known to practice intense visualization of the sport they are about to compete in, in order to win. In one experiment, researchers used EMG equipment (electromyography) to give a real-time picture of what was happening in the brain of athletes. The EMG readout of a skier focusing on and mentally rehearsing a downhill run showed the brain telling the muscles to do exactly what they would do in an actual run. This was also verified in similar EEG experiments. The conclusion drawn is that focused imagination produces the same neural results as the activity itself.[lxx]

The following excerpts are from other studies done using meticulous scientific protocols:

The kinds of vivid visualization techniques used by athletes are also highly effective in treating illness. Patients have boosted treatment of an array of acute and chronic conditions, from coronary artery disease and high blood pressure to low-back pain and musculoskeletal diseases, including fibromyalgia, by using mental pictures or metaphoric representations of their bodies fighting the illness. Visualization has also improved postsurgical outcomes, helped with pain management, and minimized the side effects of chemotherapy. Indeed, the outcome of a patient's illness has been predicted by examining the types of visualizations used to combat it. Psychologist Jeanne Achterberg, who healed herself of a rare cancer of the eye through imagery, went on to study a group of cancer patients who were using visualization to fight their own disease. She predicted with 93 percent accuracy which patients would completely recover and which would get worse or die, simply by examining their visualizations and rating them. Those who were successful had a greater ability to visualize vividly, with powerful imagery and symbols, and could hold a clear visual intention imagining themselves overpowering the cancer and the medical treatment being effective. The successful patients also practiced their visualizations regularly. **If the brain cannot distinguish between a thought and an action, would the body follow mental instructions of any sort?** If I send my body a mental intention to calm down or speed up, will it necessarily listen to me? Literature about biofeedback and mind–body medicine indicates that it will. In 1961, Neal Miller, a behavioral neuroscientist at Yale University, first proposed that people can be taught to mentally influence their autonomic nervous system and control mechanisms such as blood pressure and bowel movements, much as a child learns to ride a bicycle. He conducted a series of remarkable conditioning-and-reward experiments on rats. Miller discovered that if he stimulated the pleasure center in the brain, his rats could be trained to decrease their heart rate at will, control the rate at which urine filled their kidneys, even create different dilations in the blood vessels of each ear. If relatively simple animals like rats could achieve this remarkable level of internal control, Miller figured, couldn't human beings, with their greater intelligence, regulate more bodily processes?[lxxi]

Do you understand what she is saying? We have the power to heal through intention alone, or as a complementary to other therapies. That is how powerful our mind and imagination are. God made us in His image and likeness, He made our bodies to self-heal and our thoughts are powerful enough to tell our body what to do. Here is a specific example of the power of the mind:

One dramatic example of the power of mental suggestion concerned a small group of people with a mysterious congenital illness called ichthyosi-form erythroderma, known disparagingly as fish-skin disease because unsightly fish-like scales cover most of the body. In one study, five patients were hypnotized and told to focus on a part of their body and visualize the skin becoming normal. Within just a few weeks, 80 percent of each patient's body had completely healed. The skin remained smooth and clear.[lxxii]

Healing occurred just by focused intention.

The field of medicine has recognized something called the placebo effect for many years. Medical schools will acknowledge its existence, but not spend time teaching on how it works or how to activate it. They see it as a thorn in the efficacy of the meds they are convinced are the solution for the illness being treated.

The placebo effect has shown that beliefs are powerful, even when the belief is false. The placebo is a form of intention—an instance of intention trickery. When a doctor gives a patient a placebo, or sugar pill, he or she is counting on the patient's belief that the drug will work. It is well documented that belief in a placebo will create the same physiological effects as that of an active agent—so much so that it causes the pharmaceutical industry enormous difficulty when designing drug trials. So many patients receive the same relief and even the same side effects with a placebo as with the drug itself that a placebo is not a true

control. Our bodies do not distinguish between a chemical pro-
cess and the thought of a chemical process. Indeed, a recent
analysis of 46,000 heart patients, half of whom were taking a
placebo, made the astonishing discovery that patients taking a
placebo fared as well as those on the heart drug.[lxxiii]

The effectiveness of our intention correlates to how much we have raised our vibration and developed the power of focused intention. This is where the problem lies for many of us. Our current world is so full of distractions and busyness, we have lost the ability to focus as a culture. Even more so now in the electronic-and-entertainment-addicted society that is our world. We, even as Christians, have lost the ability to practice calming, stilling, meditating, and contemplating.

There are many ways to facilitate an improvement in the power of our focused intention without moving to a remote mountain and becoming a monk. Practicing the vibration-raising suggestions in this book is one practical way you can see results. Autogenic training, meditation, and guided imagery practices are other ways to develop the neural pathways needed to focus.[lxxiv] Be careful to choose exercises that bring your focus on the trinity and not another being. When we go to a state of alpha brain waves, we are vulnerable spiritually. According to research thoroughly evaluated by McTaggart, engaging in specific imaginations by using all of your senses, and then adding emotions, creates a neural image of that being truth as if it were actual experience. Because this image feels like an actual experience in your brain, it creates a belief in the subconscious. The best time to practice this is as you begin to wake up or just before falling asleep, when your brain waves are mostly at rest (theta waves) and in one of the best states for reprogramming.

When I interview Christians, I find most of them admitting that they struggle staying focused in prayer. Developing the brain's ability to focus has to be intentional and time has to be made to do this; it is not automatic. Past cultures were better at focus practices because of less distracted lifestyles. Our current focus is weakened by ever-growing distractions and technology. Cultures that practice meditation, stillness, and the other skills discussed have generally greater health than other cultures who don't.[lxxv]

A popular experiment by Dr. Emoto that has been replicated around the world is the rice experiment. I have seen the actual results of this experiment firsthand. Rice is cooked and put in two identical empty peanut butter jars. "Hate Ugly" is written on one and "Love Beauty" is written on the other. The two jars are then separated from one another in various parts of the house/research facility. Every day, the researcher looks at each jar and feels the words that are written on them. After three weeks, the "Love Beauty" jar of rice will still be white and the "Hate Ugly" jar of rice turns black.

When I am conducting a workshop on the Biblical roots of quantum physics, I typically do group intention demonstrations to illustrate the power of intention. One of the demonstrations is to muscle test one of my students with their back to a screen, blocking their view of the screen, but not the view of the rest of the people in the room. I will close my eyes and remain neutral or look down. I will then project either an ugly, negative picture or a beautiful, positive picture on the screen for the rest of the room to see while muscle testing the participant who cannot view the screen. Every time, the participant not viewing the screen will test strong when the beautiful picture is displayed and weak when the negative one is displayed. I will then post a mixed version of four pictures with beautiful on the left and ugly on the right and vice versa. Whatever pictures are on the left of the screen seems to determine the response of the participant's muscles. This is because our right brain (which is connected to our left eye) is dominant over our left brain (which is connected to our right eye) and emotion governs logic in initial response and energetic reaction.

The majority of Dr Emoto's water experiments involved close proximity intention, but some involved remote intention such as the experiment in which he had 500 people send positive intentions to a vial of water. He found it took a minimum of fifty people to make a notable impact on the vial of water. When the intention was specific to a certain amount of known data and specific outcomes, there were statistically significant results. Perhaps the most fascinating experiments in intention and quantum physics' law of non-locality had to do with time and took place thousands of years ago.

Jesus Healed Back Through Space and Time

In her CD series, "In the Midst," Christian preacher Katie Souza teaches on a fascinating word study done throughout the gospels. I highly recommend the purchase of this teaching as I have never heard anyone else teach on this exact topic, and the CD set goes into much more depth than I am about to in this book.

To summarize, wherever you see the words translated as "in the midst" in the Bible, you will find some kind of supernatural occurrence. These words actually make reference to a rip or tear in the fabric of space and time. So in Matthew 3:17, for example, when the sky opens and a dove appears and you hear the voice say, "This is my son in whom I am well-pleased," you will see the words "in the midst."

As it turns out, every time Jesus healed someone, the words "in the midst" are present in the original language. So, miracles happen as some kind of quantum leap through space from the dimension of Heaven. There is another word used in the examples of Jesus healing. The original word is "eck" which means "back to origins." An example of this is the story of the man with the withered hand seen in Mark 3:1-6. When Jesus says, "stretch forth," the word "eck" is present in the original language. Another example is seen in the story of blind Bartimaeus when Jesus mentions that he is the "son of Timaeus" (Mark 10:46-52).As we discussed earlier, "Timaeus" means "idol worshipper" and it was believed that the worship of idols (statues that have no sight, hearing, or speaking abilities) was the demonic cause of blindness, deafness, and being mute. The word "eck" and the phrase "in the midst" are present. In both of these cases, Jesus is traveling through the fabric of space and time ("in the midst") to the "eck" (origin or cause) and removing the cause.

If we go back in time through the quantum dimension and remove the cause, the result is the removal of the consequence that came from that cause. Both healings were results of something their ancestors had done, causing their descendants a crippled hand and blindness. Jesus didn't just do a miracle, He went back in time with powerful intention and removed the original cause.

Earlier we talked about entrainment and scriptures supporting entrainment. In Matthew 18:19-20 (ESV), it says:

> "[19]Again I say to you, that if two of you agree on earth about anything that they may ask, it shall be done for them by My Father who is in heaven. [20]For where two or three have gathered together in My name, I am there in their midst."

So, if we are entrained when we gather in unity, even with just one other person, Jesus comes through space and time to be with us.

When I use muscle testing to go back into someone's past, in essence, we are going back through the fabric of space and time and energetically removing the emotion, belief, sin of the ancestor, trauma, etc. using prayer or a release technique. This is the model Jesus used to heal. The Bible gives us cues on how quantum physics works. We have accepted the supernatural as miraculous, but there is actual science behind what caused those miracles.

Intention can change the past, which changes the present and future. But remember, the effectiveness is entirely dependent on the skill of those who had learned to focus their intention energy. When we are aligned with the Holy Spirit in power, have learned to train our intention, and raised our frequency, we walk in Biblical power. Then, when we join with others at the same frequency and entrain, imagine what can happen!

Jahn and Dunne from the Princeton Engineering Anomalies Research (PEAR) lab conducted thousands of experiments over several years testing if focused intention could influence the outcome on machines, specifically Random Event Generators (REGS), in what would eventually be termed "retrocausation." The question they sought to answer was: could focused intention *today* affect a past event and would there be a way to objectively measure this?

Volunteers were asked to mentally influence the 'heads' or 'tails' random output of REGS in a specific direction anywhere from 3 days to 2 weeks AFTER the machines had run. The results of retrocausation in 87,000 experiments were statistically significant. In fact, the results of time-displaced studies seemed to indicate that intention has greater power when outside of space/time.[lxxvi]

Another experiment outlined by McTaggart during a lecture on dealing with "retrocausation" in healing intention went as follows:

Leonard Leibovici, an Israeli professor of internal medicine in Israel and expert on hospital-acquired infections, conducted a study of healing prayer's effect on nearly 4,000 adults who had developed sepsis while in the hospital. He set up a strict protocol, using a random number generator to randomize the participants into two groups, only one of which would be prayed for, and throughout the study maintained impeccable blinding; neither the patients nor the hospital staff knew who was getting treated—or indeed even knew that a study was being car-

ried out. The names of all those in the treatment group were then handed to an individual, who said a short prayer for the well-being and full recovery of the treated group as a whole. Leibovici was interested in comparing three outcomes between the prayed-for and not-prayed-for groups: the number of deaths in the hospital; the overall length of stay in the hospital; and the duration of fever. When calculating the results, he was careful to employ several statistical measurements to examine the significance of any differences. As it happened, the group that had been prayed for suffered fewer deaths than the controls (28.1 versus 30.2 percent), although the difference was not statistically significant. What was scientifically significant, however, was the major difference between the prayed-for group and the controls related to the severity of illness and the time it took to heal. Those being prayed for had a far shorter duration of fever and hospital stay and, in general, got better faster than the controls. The subject of Leibovici's research—the healing effects of prayer—of course was hardly new. But his study offered one novel twist. The patients had been in the hospital between 1990 and 1996. The praying was carried out in 2000—between four and ten years later.[lxxvii]

These are just a few examples that prove prayer actually exists outside of time. But, not all prayers are answered. We discussed earlier some of the criteria for prayers to have effect. Jesus and Paul linked fear (low frequency emotion) to prayers being ineffective. When we are at a higher frequency, our prayers have significantly more power. If those people, who have harnessed the power of focused intention without having a relationship with Jesus or the power of the Holy Spirit, can have statistically significant outcomes, imagine how much power a Christian, who is infused with the power of the Holy Spirit, would produce when his own intention aligns with the frequency of the kingdom of God. Our subconscious, buried fears, and negative trapped emotions block faith, peace, joy, and the power that Jesus has promised to us.

Collective or Group Intention Experiments.

In addition to the random number experiment and the AIDS experiment, many other intention experiments have been done over the past few decades. The Global Consciousness Project exists to measure the impact of collective intention in order to scientifically determine if there is an impact at all. Experiments using Random Event Generators (REGs) have helped to extract order out of what seems like randomness. In short, the REGs measure the consistency of electric waves. Just before 9/11, the REGs aligned, picking up on the corporate energy of what was being planned by terrorists. When there are strong feelings of unity or division, there are statistical results in the REGs. Further experiments have shown that when groups of people came together, and were able to actually focus on the same thing with positive emotion, they could collectively affect an outcome. REGs have even shown harmony during the Super Bowl.[lxxviii]

Other studies have been conducted across the U.S. relating to crime rate. Experts intended to prove that if just 1% of the population in a given area was entrained in focused intention (prayer) on specific outcomes, there would be a statistically significant result.

One study of 24 U.S. cities showed that whenever a city reached a point where 1 percent of the population was carrying out regular focused meditation, the crime rate dropped to 24 percent. In a follow-up study of 48 cities, those 24 cities with the requisite threshold percentages of meditators (1 percent of the population) experienced a 22 percent decrease in crime, and an 89 percent reduction in the crime trend. In the other 24 cities without the threshold percentage of meditators, crime increased by 2 percent and the crime trend by 53 percent.[lxxix]

So, if a certain percentage of people (who are skilled in focused intention) vibrate at a high frequency and in unity/entrainment, then they can manifest statistically significant outcomes and set solution-based intentions in motion.

The following is a famous study which accidentally discovered an example of collective consciousness. This study is known as the "100th Monkey Effect:"

As the below article details, the 100th monkey effect is an accidental discovery by a team of researchers in the mid 1960's. The team was studying the Japanese Macaca monkey that was provided sweet potatoes from the team that they enjoyed eating. Here is an excerpt from the accounting below:

In 1952, on the island of Koshima, scientists were providing monkeys with sweet potatoes dropped in the sand. The monkeys liked the taste of the raw sweet potatoes, but they found the dirt unpleasant. An 18-month-old female named Imo found she could solve the problem by washing the potatoes in a near-by stream. She taught this trick to her mother. Her playmates also learned this new way and they taught their mothers too.
*This cultural innovation was gradually picked up by various monkeys before the eyes of the scientists. Between 1952 and 1958 all the young monkeys learned to wash the sandy sweet potatoes to make them more palatable. **Only the adults who imitated their children learned this social improvement.** Other adults kept eating the dirty sweet potatoes. Then something startling took place. In the autumn of 1958, a certain number of Koshima monkeys were washing sweet potatoes — the exact number is not known. Let us suppose that when the sun rose one morning there were 99 monkeys on Koshima Island who had learned to wash their sweet potatoes. Let's further suppose that later that morning, the hundredth monkey learned to wash potatoes. Then it happened! By that evening **almost everyone** in the tribe was washing sweet potatoes before eating them.*
The added energy of this hundredth monkey somehow created an ideological breakthrough! But notice. A most surprising

thing observed by these scientists was that the habit of washing sweet potatoes **then jumped over the sea–** Colonies of monkeys on other islands and the mainland troop of monkeys at Takasakiyama began washing their sweet potatoes.

And here is the most revealing passage:

The new behavior pattern spread to most, **but not all**, of the monkeys. **Older monkeys, in particular, remained steadfast in their established behavior patterns and resisted change.** When the new behavior pattern suddenly appeared among monkey troupes on other islands, **only a few monkeys on those islands picked up on the new idea.** The ones most receptive to new ideas started imitating the new behavior and demonstrating it to the impressionable younger ones. **Thus, they too began their own path towards their eventual hundredth monkey effect.**

First the effect was not a complete and total paradigm shift within the monkey population. At best, all that occurred was a transition of awareness; the newer monkeys learned about the washing method, but did not automatically begin washing the potatoes.

Second, the transmission occurred after a sufficient number of monkeys in the host population expressed the washing behavior. It was then that "only a few monkeys on those [new] islands" began washing the potatoes. In other words, it wasn't enough to simply be aware of this new way, it had to be accepted and expressed in order to 'build up' in the host population, which eventually experienced a pandemic awareness of the better way.

Finally, the newly affected monkeys on the surrounding islands "began their own path towards their eventual hundredth monkey effect," in other words, that the affected population had a time delay between transmission and the majority of monkeys displaying the washing behavior.

All of these points suggest an entrainment or synchronization

process, which is a property of waveforms or systems of frequen-
cy. The mind and consciousness have long been associated to
frequency and rhythmic patterns, and this transmission effect
perfectly matches what can be observed in other phenomenon,
such as synchronizing metronomes.

When two systems of motion come in contact with each other,
such that information from one can be transmitted to the other,
a slow and steady process of entrainment takes place. Eventu-
ally the two different systems synchronize to the point that the
motion of one is reflective of the other.[lxxx]

Remember the metronome experiment discussed earlier? It showed how metronomes in close proximity synchronize in a short period of time. This observation showed that proximity did not limit the effects of the waves in entrainment. This points to non-locality or entanglement in quantum physics.

Recent studies show that happiness in the workplace has a direct effect on success and productivity in corporate culture. Remember the entrainment and synchronizing examples? When the bulk of energy in a community is positive, the vibration of that entire culture is higher.[lxxxi]

Have you ever noticed trends that seemed to spring up overnight? Suddenly, there is a vape store on every corner. Suddenly, every kid has to have the same toy or pair of Nikes. These can be explained by principles of entanglement/non-locality which state that protons are connected outside of space and time and affect each other. This is what allows our prayers to reach the other side of the world. This can be the explanation to many "coincidences" and is also proof we are all connected. What the individual does, thinks, and says affects the whole. If we truly grasped how what we do affects each other and how much power there is in unity, we may be more inclined to make corporate unity and focus a priority. We would resolve disputes quickly and understand why New Testament scripture stresses conflict resolution, not judging, and dwelling in unity, peace, and joy. 1 Corinthians 12:14-20 (NASB) says:

¹⁴For the body is not one member, but many. ¹⁵If the foot says, 'Because I am not a hand, I am not a part of the body,' it is not for this reason any the less a part of the body. ¹⁶And if the ear says, 'Because I am not an eye, I am not a part of the body,' it is not for this reason any the less a part of the body. ¹⁷If the whole body were an eye, where would the hearing be? If the whole were hearing, where would the sense of smell be? ¹⁸But now God has placed the members, each one of them, in the body, just as He desired. ¹⁹If they were all one member, where would the body be? ²⁰But now there are many members, but one body.

Romans 12:4-5 reads:
⁴For just as we have many members in one body and all the members do not have the same function, ⁵so we, who are many, are one body in Christ, and individually members one of another.

Galatians 5:9 says:
A little leaven leavens the whole lump of dough.

These experiments are some of many that confirm the idea of collective frequency or vibration creating collective consciousness. Those who understand this and seek to bring destruction know how creating chaos and violence can "leaven" the whole batch and create collective hatred. But, the same principles can be used to raise the collective vibration of the world towards love. Even though McTaggart is not a professing Christian, the encouragement of an international movement towards positive collective intention is certainly a role model paradigm for the body of Christ if we would make unity a priority.

The Application for Corporate Culture

One of the industries that has failed to apply quantum physics principles into their production is corporate America. While many companies invest time, money, and energy into consultants and innovators whose jobs are to improve the corporate environment, there is still a great deficit in the understanding of entrainment, the power of intention, and the effects these principles could have on the corporate environment. Companies that promote wellness, benefits, and pro-employee services, have statistically less turnover, better employee production, less employee illness, and overall better satisfaction ratings and reviews. Essentially, what these companies have learned is that the application of energy principles are the best investment for better corporate cultures.

I have found that many of my clients suffering from mental/emotional stress and physical illnesses work in an emotionally and/or physically toxic environment. I have had clients who present with migraines, autoimmune pain, and allergies test positive for mold in their systems due to an environmental exposure at work. Clients struggling with emotional stress will report having toxic, condescending, abusive, or cruel managers and bosses who don't seem to value their input or constructive criticism. When the employee feels disempowered and helpless against a condescending, controlling, or outright abusive boss, they will often manifest physical and emotional illnesses that can, in extreme cases, cause them to quit. Recently, one of my clients passed away from cancer. It was later revealed the location of their employment for thirty years had untreated asbestos that most certainly led to the health issues and death of my client.

Imagine the improvements in mental, emotional, physical, and spiritual health if corporations made health a priority in the structure of their business. The principles in this book can be applied to alter the energy field inside the corporate environment. Imagine entraining with a leader who has a high frequency and who chooses to expand positive solutions versus criticism and pessimism. Imagine wellness and higher energy among employees and structures in place of confronting abusive, condescending, and toxic behaviors that cause the destructive energies in daily interactions.

In an experiment with plants, a measurement device was connected to plants through water, allowing the plants' frequency to show differential measurements on a screen. In the same room, living Krill-like

162

organisms were thrown into boiling water. Immediately, the plants on the other side of the room measured distress. Evidence that all plant life is connected was shown in this and many other experiments with even the most simplistic plant life. Somehow, the krill's distressed energy was immediately connected to the plants'. These measurements not only proved that all plant life is connected, but showed that all living organisms are connected. Imagine, then, the impact on the human energy when another person is highly distressed or harmed. If a boss verbally berates an employee in front of other people, their energy would be greatly diminished and emit distressed vibrations. While fear and intimidation tactics have previously been thought to be motivating and productive, quantum physics vehemently disagrees.

Many studies have been carried out to find what makes companies, sports teams, athletes, politicians, entertainers, and the like succeed or fail. In *Power vs Force*, Dr. Hawkins uses multiple examples of success, but presents them from the lens of the impact on higher frequency environments. He points to the factors in each example that show a higher frequency more consistent with joy, peace, courage, collective pride, and other positive states of being as compared to fear, shame, anger, frustration, guilt, or negative states of being. His purpose in writing this book was to demonstrate that when groups entrain collectively in positive states, they generate a more positive field of vibration that affects all those around. We see a classic example of this in the stereotypical locker room pep talk prior to a team going out on the field. This concept also affirms the existence of cheerleaders and why sports teams are known to play better on their home field (more positive energy in support of them).[lxxxii]

There is a great deal of compelling science and research that proves living in a state of high frequency, love, joy, peace, courage, acceptance, and so on creates a positive attractor field which draws entrainment. If our world truly grasped this overwhelming evidence and we practiced it, everyday life would look very different in all arenas.

CHAPTER 15
YOU CAN CHANGE THE WORLD

"**H**eaven is my throne and the earth is my footstool. Where, then in a house that you could build for Me? And where will My resting place be?" Isaiah 66:1, Acts 7:49

If the kingdom of God is peace and joy, then He must dwell in peace and joy. I often find myself singing this wonderful Vineyard Song from a few decades ago called "Resting Place." Here is a snippet of the lyrics:

Here, oh Lord, have I prepared for you a home, long have I desired for you to dwell. Here, oh Lord, have I prepared a resting place. Here, oh Lord, I wait for you alone.

I have heard and seen many Christians sincerely desire to be a resting place and tabernacle for the Lord. The criteria for the Holy Spirit to dwell in us is the frequency of Romans 14:17. Righteousness is found in the cross, in peace, and in joy. (It is *not* found in striving.) The character, nature, and frequency of the Holy Spirit is the same frequency as the kingdom. If we are consumed by fear, worry, doubt, conflict, unforgiveness, resentment, and many unresolved, trapped emotions/beliefs that do not align with His truth, we cannot be a resting place. Being a resting place is a state of being, a frequency. It is the most important place we can be for Him to make His home in us.

Have you ever been in a large crowd that made you feel small and insignificant? I believe all of our hearts cry out to be significant, to matter, to have worth and value. I have often wondered what difference I can truly make in the world. I realize I am important to my children and my friends. I realize that in my ministry experience and profession, God has used me to impact people's lives in a positive way. All of this feels really good, but that good feeling fades quickly as I realize past successes never satisfy for long in this linear timeline. The only true, consistent experience is being a resting place for the Holy Spirit.

A decade ago, there was a TV series called "Heroes." One of the main characters was named "Claire" who was played by the actress Hayden Panettiere. Claire was a teenager who could self-heal and was practically immortal with the only exception being head injuries. In the fall of 2007, the catch-phrase advertising for the show was, "Save the cheerleader, save the world." This phrase made reference to the story line that somehow Claire would "save the world" and must be protected at all costs.

As I was preparing the first edition of this book, I thought about that catch phrase. What is a cheerleader? A cheerleader is someone who doesn't look at the reality of a situation (i.e., the football game) and whose job it is to speak possibility with great enthusiasm. She/he is, in fact, a Pollyanna whose job is to stay positive and never give up hope. Cheerleaders speak blessings and victory. They do not judge the character or performance of their team, they only encourage and speak possibilities. They practice the law of expansion as a rule.

I believe that this phrase is a prophetic call to the body of Christ. Each one of us has an inner cheerleader somewhere inside. If you believe that the principles of quantum physics are true, then imagine the personal implications if you truly practiced it. What if we deliberately took our thoughts captive (2 Corinthians 10:5) and practiced Philippians 4:8, only thinking on good things? Imagine if we stopped several times a day and truly repented for judging others (and not just strangers, but politicians, preachers, our parents, our kids, etc.). What if we made the conscious choice to bless them instead of judging them? Can you imagine what your life would be like if your root issues, emotions, and irrational belief systems were exposed and transformed? What if your attitude was focused on God's transformational process in your life? Imagine spending your time visualizing a world full of God's love, peace, and power (like a cheerleader) instead of focusing on all the evil in the world. The evil does need to be exposed, but it needs to be done so while focusing on real and active solutions, or we only create despair. I am not suggesting denial, but an awareness of how much time we spend each day focused on thinking positive thoughts. At any given time, there are both powerfully good and powerfully evil things going on in the world. What if we exposed and acknowledged the evil, but focused on the good, holding the faith and evidence that God is a transformational God? What if we believed He could truly take away pain and suffering and turn what the enemy meant for evil into something powerful?

What if we took seriously the lifestyle issues addressed in the previous chapters? What if we joined with high frequency people, asked Jesus to be "in the midst," and entrained/focused our intentions on specific outcomes through prayer? If we successfully did this, even 51% of the time, I believe the following would result:

- We would stay in a state of joy and peace which is the kingdom of God. All our needs would be met. We would enjoy each day to the fullest because we are not worrying about tomorrow.
- We would be in God's will according to Ephesians 5:17-20.
- By quickly taking negative thoughts about others captive and choosing to bless them, we would reap blessing and not the law of bitter root judgments. There would be less "bad fruit" in our lives.
- By thinking only positive thoughts about ourselves, we would move towards believing we are sons and not slaves. Remember, sons walk in God's authority, manifesting the signs and wonders of the glory of God.
- By practicing the technique of visualization and focusing our attention and intention or prayer on the solution and not the problem (law of expansion), we could manifest a world that is full of God's Holy Spirit, righteousness, and peace. What we give energy to expands and grows. (By focusing on, talking about, and thinking about the evil in the world, we bring our vibration down, giving energy to and empowering evil.)

- Because we are all interconnected, our higher vibration could raise the vibration of the whole world. One individual matters. Being conscious of how our vibrations can impact those around us could be more productive because we would be entraining or synchronizing their energy to our higher vibration.
- We would indeed be resting places or homes for the Holy Spirit to dwell.

According to Trudeau's teachings in "Your Wish is my Command," all of the "secret societies" have known this information for decades and practice it as a means of securing and maintaining wealth. These groups are not professing Christians and serve other gods (Lucifer). Do you understand what this means? The followers of other gods, not the one, true Lord Jesus, have mastered the art of "prayer" (thought, intention, visualizing) and practice it as part of their lifestyle. They expect this application of the law of attraction to work for them on a regular basis and it does. Most of them have greater faith in "the universe" (via the law of attraction) than the church has in a loving God. The one thing these groups lack is the supernatural power of the cross to exert forgiveness and love from the spirit and, most importantly, a real relationship with a living God. WAKE UP believers! We have access to the most high God through prayer, thought, and intention. We have the power and authority to change the world as sons of the one and only king. We are not using this power effectively as a whole. By taking on these truths, we get to be participants in the greatest move of God in history.

Imagine if believers all over the world took the scriptures I have discussed in this book seriously and made Philippians 4:6-8, Ephesians 5:17-20, Matthew 7:1, and 2 Corinthians 10:5 a priority each day. What do you think we, as a unified corporate body, could manifest in the world? The unity of believers is the constant target of Satan's attacks because he knows the truths mentioned in this book and The Book to be true. Individually, if we were determined to walk in love for God, ourselves, and others (by practicing these scriptures; releasing our trapped emotions, traumas, judgments and vows; forgiving and blessing quickly; and walking as sons of a living God) we would truly change the world. God tells us throughout scripture that we have the power and authority to change the world. What if you practiced the vibration-raising suggestions in this book? What would it be like to vibrate at peace and joy?

Often, people don't understand why they should go back through their life and review their history. Critics often call this "navel gazing" because it requires intense inward focus. Sons of the king know they will rule one day and by living their lives with this in mind, they aspire to become the best rulers they can become. They are more concerned with who they are than what they do. We must embrace a life paradigm that involves allowing our wounds to be triggered in order to reveal where our subconscious (and conscious) beliefs do not align with God's word. This creates a life of constant transformation and the ability to see all occurrences as potential for transformation and blessing. Ironically, many of the critics in our lives have had truly painful childhoods, but they don't want to revisit any of it. We are all creatures of God's light and the Holy Spirit; all the trapped emotions inside us lower the intensity of our light in daily interaction. Under the power of the anointing we may shine brightly, but in the context of our day-to-day relationships, we stay in fleshly coping mechanisms because our wounds are being triggered daily by life's events.

Maybe Mark Twain had more of a clue about God than he has been accredited. He wrote, *"Sing like no one's listening, love like you've never been hurt, dance like nobody's watching, and live like its heaven on earth."* And I would add to this: Get busy vibrating high!

SUMMARY
A CALL TO ACTION

I have spent thirty years in an ebb-and-flow of healing and transformational processes. It has frustrated me to no end to see this process happen much more slowly than I had desired. Over the past several years, as I discovered the missing puzzle pieces discussed in this book and applied them to my life, I have truly felt an acceleration of the deep-level changes I had been seeking. Perhaps the very deepest key was realizing that, in many areas, I did not believe God or the universe was truly for me and therefore continued to expect trials, suffering, and pain. After all, Paul suffered tremendously, as do saints all over the world. I am not saying that God is not intentionally bringing us to transformation, but the topic of suffering is truly debated biblically. There are many metaphors that suggest we must go through some painful things in life to become equipped as sons of God. The Bible uses the image of gold going through fire to be purified, the image of a vine being pruned, the image of being crucified (our flesh) and many others. I also like the metaphor of the olive. The olive (us) must be pressed for the oil (the anointing) to be extracted. But when we assume that every negative thing we go through is God punishing us or causing us to suffer (like these metaphors might suggest), we lose trust in a loving Father figure. We live in low frequency fear.

It is, in my opinion, more accurate to align with the words of Jesus who paints Abba as a loving Father who wants us to thrive and live in peace and joy. Our own beliefs, traumas, generational iniquities, and the places where the enemy has access to our lives will allow us to attract or reap suffering. But even in our blind spots or ignorance of these principles, God still intends for all of our negative experiences to bring transformation and redemption if we will let them.

169

Understanding that everything that happens ultimately brings us to transformation allows us to rejoice in all things. However, I must admit, for many years I was at odds with God. How could someone who says He loves me so much allow for constant pain to occur in my life? After many hours in His presence, I drew the conclusion of Job: "Though You slay me, yet I will hope in You" (Job 13:15). I understood God to be a God of healing and had experienced the restoration of lost things and erasure of painful memories, but on a deep level, I wasn't sure I really trusted Him. I realize I had an expectation of suffering and pain, so I got what I expected. The spiritual pride in me created a belief that spiritual people suffer and only people with an important call on their life have to go through truly difficult things. But something else, deep inside me, would watch people suffer over and over and think, perhaps, God was cruel. My paradigm wasn't quite right.

Understanding the law of attraction has given me a new understanding of "ask, seek, and knock" (Matthew 7:7). Since I have chosen to believe God is for me and that I have favor with God (and men), my life has been more peaceful and I continue to move in to a deeper relationship with Him, knowing I am fulfilling His call on my life with great joy and expectation.

I invite you to reread the "To Do" list in chapter thirteen and make a strategy of change. This will require you to make time on a daily basis to practice the principles outlined in this book. Changes are best done a little at time if you want to maintain them. New Year's resolutions rarely work because our brains are not wired to accept radical change easily. Sit down and write out a three-month plan of daily, weekly, and monthly changes you want to make and *be diligent* to practice them daily. Don't give up if you miss a day or two. Talk to people you trust and ask them to hold you accountable to make these changes. Do whatever it takes to truly implement them. Read and reread this book and other similar sources to remind yourself that you believe in these spiritual laws and the law of attraction. My other book, *30 Days to Peace and Joy*, includes a journal and checklists to help you apply the principles in this book. If it only takes 1% of the population entrained at a high frequency to change an entire city, then if you, I, and other believers are the only ones to apply

170

these principles to our lives, we can truly change the world. **Would you become a cheerleader with me?**

I know the Lord downloaded this book to me as a source for the body of Christ to realize we are in a war against evil and darkness like never before. The enemy has worked for decades to block us spiritually and generationally and has influenced us to accept worldly beliefs which has watered down our authority and made us look very similar to the world. Those who belong to the New Age movement look more godly and walk in greater power than most of the church. I feel a passion and call to wake up believers to not only the concept of frequency, but to an understanding of how and why our vibration is so low and we are constantly plagued by the enemy and our own trauma. I feel the burden of educating people to understand the destructive effects of the modern world we live in and the programs that have been gradually implemented to make us blind sheep to destruction. Why does America have the highest cancer rate in the world? Why are we the most depressed, anxious, chemically imbalanced, ADD and ADHD stricken country in the world? Why are we not challenging the way we live and believe as the root causes to these issues? My short-term goal is to educate people on wellness, teach them to raise their vibration, and assist them in closing the demonic doors in their life which have dulled their spirits. My long-term goal is to create a population of mindful, high vibrational, passionate believers who walk in the authority of sonship that God intended for us.

In this next season of transformation, the outpouring of the glory of God will involve a level of power in our words and thoughts that will manifest signs, miracles, and wonders. We can disqualify ourselves by staying in a worldly mindset of judgment, gossip, and offense or we can decide we have been called and commissioned to change the world. We must stay focused on the mission to change the world through forgiveness, repentance, and blessing. We can focus on the glorious possibilities anyone can achieve and manifest in any situation when they are focused on and aligned to God. Because we know we can co-create a new reality, let's get going!

NOTES

i.   "Frequency of Human Body, EnergeticX, accessed in September 2019, https://energicxusa.com/frequency-of-human-body/.

ii.   Singh, "Consciousness and the Third Eye," SpeakingTree.In, May 30, 2012, https://www.speakingtree.in/blog/consciousness-and-the-third-eye.

iii.   Peake, "The Physics Of Consciousness: The Zero-Point Field, Pineal Gland And Out-of-Body Experience," Conscious Reminder, https://conscious-reminder.com/2017/09/08/physics-consciousness-zero-point-field-pineal-gland-body-experience/.

iv.   Zajac, "The Law of Attraction & Quantum Physics."

v.   Trudeau, *Your Wish Is Your Command,* CD 1 Track 2.

vi.   healthyself, "Electromagnetic Frequencies," *The Frequency of the Human Body and Your Coffee,* last modified on September 17, 2006, http://cellphonesafety.wordpress.com/2006/09/17/the-frequency-of-the-human-body-and-your-coffee/.

vii.   Hawkins, *Power vs. Force.*

viii.   Emoto, "Words Have Power," photograph, accessed in 2013, http://archive.constantcontact.com/fs190/1109404269370/archive/1112713335901.html.

ix.   Beckler, "High Vibration Foods to Elevate Your Consciousness," Ask-Angels.com, 2018, https://www.ask-angels.com/spiritual-guidance/high-vibration-foods/m.

x.   Byrne, *The Secret.*

xi.   Byrne, *The Secret.*

xii.   Trudeau, *Your Wish Is Your Command,* CD 1 Track 4.

xiii.   Trudeau, *Your Wish Is Your Command,* CD 1 Track 5.

xiv.   Allen, *As a Man Thinketh.*

xv.   "Butterfly effect," Wikipedia, last modified on May 12, 2020, https://en.wikipedia.org/wiki/Butterfly_effect.

xvi.   Bollow, "How Fast Is Your Brain?"

xvii.   McLeod, "Freud and the Unconscious Mind."

xviii. Burriss, George, Bible Study, Munger Place Church, Dallas, 2012.

xix.   Schore, *Affect Regulation the Origin of Self: The Neurobiology of Emotional Development.*

xx.   Friesen, et al., *The Life Model: Living from the Heart Jesus Gave You: The Essentials of Christian Living.*

xxi.   "Karma," Wikipedia, last modified on February 28, 2020, https://en.wikipedia.org/wiki/Karma.

xxii.   Kirkwood, *The Power of Blessing.*

xxiii. Trudeau, *Your Wish Is Your Command,* CD 5 Tracks 4-8, CD 6, CD 7.

xxiv.   Burriss, George, Bible Study, Munger Place Church, Dallas, 2012.

xxv.   Blue Letter Bible, "hindered," https://www.blueletterbible.org/lang/Lexicon/Lexicon.cfm?strongs=G1581&t=KJV.

xxvi.   Henderson, "Operating in the Courts of Heaven: Granting God the Legal Right to Fulfill His Passion and Answer Our Prayers."

xxvii.   Leaf, *Who Switched Off my Brain,* 19-22.

xxviii.   iAwake Technologies, "The Deeper Meaning of Entrainment."

xxix.   McCollam, *God Vibrations Study Guide: A Kingdom Perspective on the Power of Sound,* 39.

xxx.   Geekologie, "100 Metronomes On A Floating Table All Synchronizing Themselves Over Time."

xxxi.   Barnatan, "Conversation with Dr. Bruce Lipton About Sound Healing," YouTube.

xxxii.   Vision Life Ministries, "Vision Life Ministries: Equipping Saints to Soar."

xxxiii.   McTaggart, *The Intention Experiment,* 3034-3044, Kindle.

xxxiv.   ZYTO, "ZYTO: Wellness Decision Support Software."

xxxv.   ASYRA, "Asyra: The World's #1 Bio-Energetic Screening System."

xxxvi.   Healy, "Das ist der Healy; Das Wearable für Gesundheit · Wohlbefinden · Balance."

xxxvii.   HUSO, "The Science of Sound."

xxxviii.   HUSO, "The Science of Sound."

xxxix.   Wholetones, "Wholetones: Michael S. Tyrell."

xl.   Ange, "WholeTones Michael S. Tyrrell: How Does It Work?,"*Carers Loft,* last modified February 26, 2016, https://carersloft.com/wholetones-michael-s-tyrrell-how-does-it-work.

xli.   EVOX Therapeutics, "EVOX Therapeutics."

xlii.   Byrne, *The Secret,* 47-48, Print.

xliii.   Sasson, "How Many Thoughts Does Your Mind Think in One Hour?"

xliv.   Kahn, "7 Scientific Reasons You Should Listen To Your Heart (Not Your Brain)."

xlv.   Burk, *Alien Human Spirit.*

xlvi.   Psychology Today, "Epigenetics," Psychology Today, April 9, 2020, https://www.psychologytoday.com/us/basics/epigenetics.

xlvii.   Fosar and Bludorf, "Scientists Prove DNA Can Be Reprogrammed by Words and Frequencies."

xlviii.   Henderson, *Operating in the Courts of Heaven.*

xlix.   Lewis, "Fearful Experiences Passed On In Mouse Families."

l.   Hamilton, "Visualisation Alters the Brain & Body."

li.   Wolynn Mark, interview by Tami Simon, *Becoming Aware of Inherited Family Trauma,* Insights at the Edge, June 25, 2019.

lii.   Jubilee Resources International Inc., "Freemasonry: Prayer of Release for Freemasons and Their Descendants."

liii.   Levy, "MTHFR Mutation Symptoms, Diagnoses & Natural Remedies."

liv.   Nicholson, Ester, "Why do secrets keep us sick?" Addiction Blog, September 1, 2013, https://addictionblog.org/spirit/why-do-secrets-keep-us-sick/.

lv.   Wright, *A More Excellent Way: Be In Health,* 125.

lvi.   Croce, "Thought Behind the Actions — What are miasms?"

lvii.   Hungerford, "Thoughts and Intents Can Reprogram Our DNA," *Healing Music Frequencies.*

lviii.   Dispenza, *Breaking the Habit of Being Yourself: How to Lose Your Mind and Create a New One,* lecture based on book published in 2013.

lix.   "Neuroplasticity," Wikipedia, last modified on May 9, 2020, https://en.wikipedia.org/wiki/Neuroplasticity.

lx.   McQueen, "Does Consciousness Cause Quantum Collapse?"

lxi.   Merriam Webster, online edition, s.v. "prodigal."

lxii.   Paul, "The Law of Attraction - It's About Frequency."

lxiii.   "Repressed memory," Wikipedia, last modified on April 5, 2020, https://en.wikipedia.org/wiki/Repressed_memory.

lxiv.   Radawan, "What is the subconscious mind?"

lxv.   Chapman, *The Five Love Languages.*

lxvi.   Loyd, *The Healing Code.*

lxvii.   "Earl Nightingale," Wikipedia, last modified on December 3, 2019, https://en.wikipedia.org/wiki/Earl_Nightingale.

lxviii.   McTaggart, *The Intention Experiment*, Kindle.

lxix.   McTaggart, *The Intention Experiment,* 1744-1766, Kindle.

lxx.   Ibid, 2588, Kindle.

lxxi.   Ibid, 2633-2657, Kindle.

lxxii.   Ibid, 2714, Kindle.

lxxiii.   Ibid, 2736-2748, Kindle.

lxxiv.   Cuncic, "Autogenic Training for Reducing Anxiety."

lxxv.   Thorpe, "12 Science-Based Benefits of Meditation."

lxxvi.   McTaggart, *The Intention Experiment,* 3170-3181, Kindle.

lxxvii.   McTaggart, Lynn, Lecture on Intention Experiments.

lxxviii. McTaggart, *The Intention Experiment,* 3470, Kindle.

lxxix.   McTaggart, The Intention Experiment, 3505, Kindle.

lxxx.   Deschamps, "The 'Human' Hundredth Monkey Effect Explained: Critical Mass, The Shift And What It Could Look Like."

lxxxi.   Craig, "2 New Studies Reinforce Why Company Culture Is So Important."

lxxxii.   Hawkins, *Power vs. Force,* Chapters 10-14.

BIBLIOGRAPHY

Allen, James. *As a Man Thinketh*. CreateSpace Independent Publishing Platform, 2010.

ASYRA. "Asyra: The World's #1 Bio-Energetic Screening System. Accessed in September 2019. https://www.asyra.co.uk/.

Barnatan, Avishai. "Conversation with Dr. Bruce Lipton About Sound Healing." YouTube. February 13, 2017. Video. https://www.youtube.com/watch?v=07MmSfo5b9U&feature=youtu.be&app=desktop.

Beckler, Melanie. "High Vibration Foods to Elevate Your Consciousness." Ask-Angels.com. https://www.ask-angels.com/spiritual-guidance/high-vibration-foods/m. 2018.

Bollow, Jeff. "How Fast Is Your Brain?" The Phenomenal Experience. Last modified in 2009. http://thephenomenalexperience.com/content/how-fast-is-your-brain/.

Burk, Arthur. *Alien Human Spirit*. Read by the author. Saphhire Leadership Group, LLC: Spartanburg, 2013. Multimedia CD series.

Byrne, Rhonda. *The Secret*. Hillsborough: Beyond Words Publishing, 2006.

Chapman, Gary. *The Five Love Languages*. Chicago: Northfield Publishing, 2010.

Craig, William. "2 New Studies Reinforce Why Company Culture Is So Important." Forbes. Last modified on December 22, 2016. https://www.forbes.com/sites/williamcraig/2016/12/22/2-new-studies-reinforce-why-company-culture-is-so-important/#558243aa7123.

Croce, Ann Jerome. "Thought Behind the Actions — What are miasms?" *National Center for Homeopathy*. Last modified September 2000. https://www.homeopathycenter.org/homeopathy-today/thought-behind-action-what-are-miasms.

Cuncic, Arlin. "Autogenic Training for Reducing Anxiety." verywellmind.com. November 29, 2019. https://www.verywellmind.com/how-to-practice-autogenic-training-for-relaxation-3024387.

Deschamps, Justin. "The 'Human' Hundredth Monkey Effect Explained | Critical Mass, The Shift And What It Could Look Like." Stillness in the Storm: An Agent of Conscious Evolution. Last modified on October 20, 2015.https://stillnessinthestorm.com/2015/10/the-human-hundredth-monkey-effec/.

EVOX Therapeutics. "EVOX Therapeutics." Accessed in September 2019. https://www.evoxtherapeutics.com/.

"Frequency of Human Body." EnergeticX. Accessed in September 2019. https://energicxusa.com/frequency-of-human-body/.

Friesen James et al. *The Life Model: Living from the Heart Jesus Gave You: The Essentials of Christian Living.* Los Angeles: Shepherds House, Inc., 2000.

Fosar, Grayzna and Bludorf, Franz. "Scientists Prove DNA Can Be Reprogrammed by Words and Frequencies." *Wake Up World.* Accessed on April 15, 2020. https://wakeup-world.com/2011/07/12/scientist-prove-dna-can-be-reprogrammed-by-words-frequencies/.

Geekologie. "100 Metronomes On A Floating Table All Synchronizing Themselves Over Time." Last modified on December 28, 2016. https://geekologie.com/2016/12/100-metronomes-on-a-floating-table-all-s.php.

Hamilton, David. "Visualisation Alters the Brain & Body." drdavidhamilton.com. Last modified on April 11, 2011. http://drdavidhamilton.com/visualisation-alters-the-brain-body/.

Hawkins, David. *Power vs. Force.* Carlsbad: Hay House Inc., 2012.

Healy. "Das ist der Healy; Das Wearable für Gesundheit · Wohlbefinden · Balance." Last modified in 2020. https://www.healyworld.net/de/partner/robinbraun.

Henderson, *Robert Operating in the Courts of Heaven.* Midlothian: Robert Henderson Ministries, 2014.

Hungerford, Del. "Thoughts and Intents Can Reprogram Our DNA." *Healing Music Frequencies.* Last modified in 2019. https://www.healingfrequenciesmusic.com/thoughts-and-intents-can-reprogram-our-dna/.

HUSO. "HUSO: Revolutionary Sound Therapy at Home." Accessed in September 2019. https://thisishuso.com/ref/53/

HUSO. "The Science of Sound." Accessed in September 2019. https://thisishuso.com/ref/53/.

iAwake Technologies. "The Deeper Meaning of Entrainment."iAwake. January 31, 2012. https://www.iawaketechnologies.com/the-deeper-meaning-of-entrainment/.

Jubilee Resources International Inc. "Freemasonry: Prayer of Release for Freemasons and Their Descendants." jubileeresources.org. Last modified in December 2014. https://jubileeresources.org/pages/freemasonry.

Kahn, Joel. "7 Scientific Reasons You Should Listen To Your Heart (Not Your Brain)." MindBodyGreen.com. Accessed in July 2019. https://www.mindbodygreen.com/0-11982/7-scientific-reasons-you-should-listen-to-your-heart-not-your-brain.html.

Kirkwood, Kerry. *The Power of Blessing*. Shippensburg: Destiny Image Publishers, Inc., 2010.

Leaf, Caroline. *Who Switched Off my Brain*. Nashville: Thomas Nelson, Inc., 2009.

Levy, Jillian. "MTHFR Mutation Symptoms, Diagnoses & Natural Remedies." Dr. Axe. July 27, 2018. https://draxe.com/health/mthfr-mutation/.

Lewis, Tanya. "Fearful Experiences Passed On In Mouse Families." LiveScience. Last modified on December 5, 2013. https://www.livescience.com/41717-mice-inherit-fear-scents-genes.html.

Loyd, Alex. *The Healing Code*. Peoria: Intermediary Publishing Group, 2010.

McCollam, Dan. *God Vibrations Study Guide: A Kingdom Perspective on the Power of Sound*. Vacaville: Sounds of the Nations, 2013.

McLeod, Saul. "Freud and the Unconscious Mind." SimplyPsychology. Last modified in 2015. https://www.simplypsychology.org/unconscious-mind.html.

McQueen, Kelvin. "Does Consciousness Cause Quantum Collapse?" Philosophy Now. 2017. https://philosophynow.org/issues/121/Does_Consciousness_Cause_Quantum_Collapse.

McTaggart, Lynn. *The Intention Experiment*. New York: Free Press, 2007. Kindle.

Paul, Margaret. "The Law of Attraction - It's About Frequency." Ezine Articles. Last modified on March 24, 2011. https://ezinearticles.com/?The-Law-of-Attraction---Its-About-Frequency&id=6111179.

Peake, Anthony. "The Physics Of Consciousness: The Zero-Point Field, Pineal Gland And Out-of-Body Experience." Conscious Reminder. https://consciousreminder.com/2017/09/08/physics-consciousness-zero-point-field-pineal-gland-body-experience/.

Psychology Today. "Epigenetics." Psychology Today. https://www.psychologytoday.com/us/basics/epigenetics. April 9, 2020.

Radawan, Farouk M. "What is the subconscious mind?" Know Myself. Accessed in September 2019. https://www.2knowmyself.com/subconscious_mind.

Sasson, Remez. "How Many Thoughts Does Your Mind Think in One Hour?" Success Consciousness. Accessed in September 2019. https://www.successconsciousness.com/blog/inner-peace/how-many-thoughts-does-your-mind-think-in-one-hour/.

Schore, Allan. *Affect Regulation the Origin of Self: The Neurobiology of Emotional Development*. Hillsborough: Lawrence Erlbaum Associates, Inc., 1994.

Singh, Virendra. "Consciousness and the Third Eye." SpeakingTree.In. May 30, 2012. https://www.speakingtree.in/blog/consciousness-and-the-third-eye.

Souza Katie. *In The Midst.* Read by the author. Katie Souza Ministries: Maricopa, 2014. Multimedia CD Series.

Thorpe, Matthew. "12 Science-Based Benefits of Meditation." Healthline. July 5, 2017. https://www.healthline.com/nutrition/12-benefits-of-meditation.

Trudeau, Kevin. *Your Wish Is Your Command.* Read by the author. Global Information Network: New York, 2009. Multimedia CD series.

Vision Life Ministries. "Vision Life Ministries: Equipping Saints to Soar." Accessed in September 2010. https://visionlife.org/.

Wholetone., "Wholetones: Michael S. Tyrell." Accessed in February 2015. https://home.wholetones.com/.

Why Don't You Try This? "Scientists Prove DNA Can Be Reprogrammed by Words and Frequencies." whydontyoutrythis.com. Last modified on June 5, 2013. http://www.whydontyoutrythis.com/2013/06/scientists-prove-dna-can-be-reprogrammed-by-words-and-frequencies.html?m=1.

Wikipedia. "Karma." Last modified on February 28, 2020. https://en.wikipedia.org/wiki/Karma.

Wolynn, Mark. *Becoming Aware of Inherited Family Trauma.* Interview by Tami Simon. Insights at the Edge, June 25, 2019.

Wright, Henry. *A More Excellent Way: Be In Health.* Pleasant Valley Publications: Thomaston, 2009.

Zajac, Walter. "The Law of Attraction & Quantum Physics." SelfGrowth.com. https://www.selfgrowth.com/articles/The_Law_of_Attraction_Quantum_Physics.html.

ZYTO. "ZYTO: Wellness Decision Support Software." Accessed in October 2019. https://www.zyto.com/.

RESOURCES

To make a personal blockage releasing appointment with Robin, visit https://www.integratedlifestrategies.com/personal-transformation.

To invite Robin to speak at your private or corporate venue or host a book signing, visit https://www.integratedlifestrategies.com/speaking-and-media.

To bring Robin in to host a retreat, visit https://www.integratedlifestrategies.com/retreats.

To view the recommended daily supplements for the average person, visit https://www.integratedlifestrategies.com/products.

To receive training on how to be an Integrated Life Practitioner and raise your vibration and that of others, go to https://www.integratedlifestrategies.com/training.

To learn about the dangers of EMF radiation and how to mitigate, protect, and heal the body from damage, visit https://www.integratedlifestrategies.com/newsletter.

I strongly believe everyone should own a "Healy" device. Owning a "Healy" will not only help you feel better and live a long, thriving life, but will help you save you money on other health products — more than paying for the cost of the device itself. To learn more about the "Healy" or to purchase the device, go to https://www.healyworld.net/de/partner/robinbraun.

ABOUT THE AUTHOR

Robin Perry Braun is also the author of *30 Days to Peace and Joy: Journey to Transformation in Daily Bite*s and *Journey Through the Storm: Overcoming the Pain of Your Husband's Porn/Sex Addiction*.

Her Certified Modality, the Integrated Life Process, is a cutting-edge holistic modality which finds, with laser precision, root issues in your life and releases them. She offers a wide variety of services from personal appointments to corporation transformation plans to workshops around the world to help equip other Certified Integrated Life Practitioners. Braun is a firm believer that businesses and churches can experience renewal when their core leadership goes through personal and corporate intensives. Participants in her corporate workshops are shown how their beliefs, judgments, and trapped emotions affect their personal life and the whole based on the spiritual principles of leadership.

Braun is available to speak for church services, retreats, and private or public book signings. Topics can be tailored to the purposes of the meeting. Contact is available on her website or by emailing her at: integratedlifestrategies@gmail.com.

To learn more about Robin Perry Braun's training services, products, or to subscribe for updates, visit www.integratedlifestrategies.com. To connect with Robin Perry Braun on social media, visit https://www.facebook.com/Integratedlifestrategies/.

TO FIND OUT MORE ABOUT THE AUTHOR, GO TO
INTEGRATEDLIFESTRATEGIES.COM.

OTHER BOOKS BY ROBIN PERRY BRAUN

30 Days To Peace & Joy: Journey To Transformation in Daily Bites
ISBN: 978-0692289600

Most people spend their lives looking for peace and joy. Did you know that you were wired for peace and joy and this is your natural state? Take a journey to transform your level of peace and joy in just 30 days. Learn tools to change your life permanently in this daily progressive transformation tool. This sequel to *A Believers Guide to the Law of Attraction* takes biblical truths and life truths and gives you practical applications that are doable. Many have made this journey and can attest to the value of these principles when applied to daily living.

Journey Through the Storm: Overcoming the Pain of Your Husband's Porn/Sex Addiction
ISBN: 978-1533591555

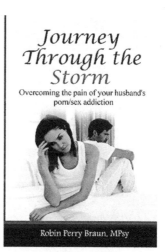

65% of today's men look at porn. Many of these married men also seek experiences outside of the marriage. The impact on the wife and family is often devastating. *Through the Storm* addresses the painful impact of sexual addiction on the wife. Real stories of real women give an authentic and tangible expression of the struggles of these wives. Practical advice is given, along with ways to find transformation through this pain. Ultimately, the goal of this journey is to find a life of peace and joy through transformation, as well as a powerful connection to a loving God.

Made in the USA
Coppell, TX
13 September 2024

37174653R10105